"I first knew Carey Casey as a young man, preparing to attend seminary, and have always had the greatest admiration for him. He has a deep love for people and a desire to lead them, especially young men, to Christ. I would highly commend to you any book written by Carey Casey."

—BILLY GRAHAM

"Carey Casey hits it out of the ballpark in his new book, *Championship Fathering*. This volume is chock full of practical information, exhortations, and examples from his own personal experience as a son and father. Perhaps most helpful is hearing about the simple yet profound ways that values were 'caught' in Carey's life and in the lives of his children. I encourage every father or father-to-be—especially those among us who lacked a strong male role model growing up—to pick up this resource and heed its God-given wisdom."

—JIM DALY
President, Focus on the Family

"I've known Carey Casey for 30 years. He's truly one of America's most respected and trusted leaders. In *Championship Fathering*, Carey lays out three easy-to-follow, fundamental steps that will take every dad in the direction his kids and wife desperately need him to go. Carey is a true example. He is a fantastic dad and speaker and he loves God devoutly."

—JOE WHITE
Founder of Kanakuk Kamps
and author of *Sticking with Your Teen*

"In *Championship Fathering*, Carey Casey lays out a vision for every dad—and for our nation. Having known him for 25 years, it is no surprise that Carey makes it plain for all dads. He brings the research-based principles of the National Center for Fathering to life with practical ideas that all of us dads can use—regardless of our circumstances. Carey shows us that we *can* win this battle for our children's future, and *yes*, that we *can* change the culture of fathering in our nation by living out the basics of Championship Fathering."

—Dr. Tony Evans
Senior Pastor, Oak Cliff Bible Fellowship
Dallas, Texas

"I met Carey Casey when he was an 18-year-old running back playing against my team for the Virginia state high school football championship. Today, Carey and I are on the same team seeking a more important championship. This is our playbook. I hope you'll join our team as we seek to become Championship Fathers."

—Coach Herman Boone
Head Coach, T.C. Williams Titans
As dramatized in the film *Remember the Titans*

"Fathers today need coaches who equip them to be effective dads. Carey Casey wants to be your coach for a championship season. I want to encourage you to get this book and join his team."

—Dr. Dennis Rainey
President, Family Life

"Winning the Heisman Trophy and being an All-Pro Receiver are great honors, but my lifelong goal is to have my children tell me I've been a Championship Father for them. Carey Casey has provided me—and you—with a great game plan to achieve that goal. If you want to be the dad your children need, *Championship Fathering* will help you get over the goal line."

—Tim Brown
Former NFL All-Pro Receiver and Heisman Trophy winner

CHAMPIONSHIP FATHERING

How to Win at Being a Dad

CAREY CASEY
WITH NEIL WILSON

TYNDALE HOUSE PUBLISHERS, INC.

CAROL STREAM, ILLINOIS

ISBN: 978-1-58997-534-7

Library of Congress Cataloging-in-Publication Data
Casey, Carey, 1955-
    Championship fathering: how to win at being a dad / Carey Casey.
        p. cm.
    "A Focus on the Family book."
    Includes bibliographical references.
    1. Fathers—Religious life. 2. Fatherhood—Religious aspects—Christianity. I. Title.
    BV4529.17.C37 2008
    248.8'421—dc22

                                                        2008040733

Printed in the United States of America
3 4 5 6 7 / 15 14 13 12 11 10 09

*This book is dedicated to my father's dreams for me,
to my father-dreams for my children,
and to the father-dreams of every dad who reads these pages.
May we be the generation that launches a culture
of Championship Fathering in our land and beyond.*

———

Contents

Acknowledgments

When you become "published," suddenly you have to be an authority on whatever your book is about. So I enter this new arena with a bit of fear and trepidation. But I also do so with a great sense of calling, because responsible Championship Fathering is so vital to our future.

As you'll see in what follows, I'm an average dad who has been blessed to have some very good people around me. When I look at what is in this book, I realize that so many people have contributed to it in one way or another.

First and foremost, I know who butters my bread, if you will. God has given me so many blessings in life, as well as the passion and vision for this work—starting even when I was a boy. For many years, I have always known that the greatest thing I can do in life is to be a man of God, a husband, and a father. That has always been part of what I wanted to do and be in life.

My parents, Ralph and Sarah Casey, inspired me and never gave up on me even when others did. I was blessed to have them there. My bride's parents, Dr. Perry and Mildred Little, were very dedicated parents and grandparents even in difficult circumstances. I thank my sister, Camellia, and my brother, Corwin, for being constant sources of support. And I'm grateful to the other members of what is, in my experience, the greatest family in the world: Melanie, my bride of more than 30 years; Christie and her husband, Shunton; Patrice, her husband, John, and my grandson, John-John; my son Marcellus, his wife, Stephanie, and our granddaughter, Salem Miel; and of course Chance, who helps me keep my fathering fresh.

I am grateful for those who serve or have served on the staff at the National Center for Fathering since my arrival—great people who work tirelessly and who have helped me learn more about myself and about fathering than I ever thought I could. My friend and partner, Peter Spokes, the president at the Center, gives me great confidence as CEO because I know he will dot all the i's and cross all the t's to keep the place running smoothly. Brock Griffin, our staff writer, helps me bring the message off the page and make it plain for our readers and radio listeners; his work shows up throughout this book. Others who have served here during my tenure include Brian Blomberg, Lucy Bloom, Cathy Henton, Amos Johnson, Ron Nichols, Maya Ostema, Bea Peters, Vera Lu Pollard, Sherri Solis, Debbi Swirczynski, George Williams, Steve Wilson, and George Young. Members of our WATCH D.O.G.S. team include Chris Danenhauer, Scott Dorf, Samuel Barnes, Frank Hannon, Shelly Perry, and Eric Snow.

We have also been blessed to have board members who have given of their time, talents, and treasure to help fulfill the mission of the National Center. Our current board members include Blake Ashdown, Ron Blain, David Carr, Steve Cox, George Garza, Dr. Peter LeDoux, Lee Paris, Mario Shane, Greg Solis, and Jason Wingard. Dr. Rich Hosley, Joel Jennings, and Sam Mathis also served on our board during my time here.

Others have helped us along the way with enthusiastic support and encouragement—including Russell Brown, Rich Hastings, Lloyd Hill, Joe Lee, Drew Maddux, Chip and Debbie Mahon, Gretchen Mahoney, Al Mueller, Kevin and Lisa Olsen, and Denny and Allyson Weinberg.

It's an honor and privilege to follow the Center's founder, Dr. Ken Canfield, a man with such passion and grace. From the Center's beginning in 1990 until the end of 2005, he raised the banner for fatherhood and prepared the way for the great things God has in store for us in the years to come.

I have had the privilege of working with quality people throughout the process of writing this book—including Steve Smith, a friend from years ago here in Kansas City, who believed a Carey Casey book was worth pursuing and promoted the idea to his colleagues at Focus on the Family. The other staff we have worked with at Focus—Larry Weeden, John Duckworth, Jim Daly, and others—have also conducted themselves with excellence and class. Thank you for seeing the need in our culture for Championship Fathers and for taking on this project. Neil Wilson of The Livingstone Corporation drew from his giftedness and passion to put my ideas into words that have real purpose and clarity. Thanks also to my friend Tony Dungy for being a great model as a father and for contributing the foreword for this book.

I am indebted to many fine people who have invested in me and who have really helped to raise my family and me. During my junior year in high school, I was introduced to a great organization called the Fellowship of Christian Athletes, and I have been associated with it in some way ever since. My lifelong friends there are too numerous to name, though I do want to mention former CEO Dal Shealy and former Dallas Cowboys Coach Tom Landry, who was very active with FCA. Coach Landry was a father figure to me, and actually passed away on the same day my own father died; both were men of God, 75 years of age, and had been married to their brides for more than 50 years. Alicia Landry is still an encouragement to our family.

Thanks to Wayne and Ann Gordon and the entire Lawndale Community Church family in Chicago. Wayne held me accountable every day to be a good husband and father while we served together there. I would also like to mention others who have invested in my life through the years: Dr. James Braxton and First Baptist Church in Salem, Virginia; the people at the Mount Hebron Baptist Church in Garland, Texas; my father in the ministry, Dr. Charles Briscoe, and Paseo Baptist Church in Kansas City; Pastor Paul Brooks and our church family at First Baptist Church Raytown; Jim Haney and the National Association of Basketball Coaches; and Coach Herm Edwards and the Kansas City Chiefs.

Thank you all. You are a great encouragement to me.

Foreword

by Tony Dungy
Head Coach, Indianapolis Colts

I remember being on the podium during the victory celebration after our team won the 2007 Super Bowl. As I stood there in the middle of all that noise and confetti, I thought about all the people who helped me along the way. Probably more than anyone else, I thought about my dad. He died in 2004, but I really wish he'd been there to celebrate with me.

I learned so many lessons from him. There were numerous times when he helped me talk through my disappointments. He attended all my games when I was growing up, but it was the experiences going to and coming from the games—riding in the car and walking back and forth to the fields—that have really stuck with me. We would talk about everyday issues and questions, and often more important topics would come up—like academics, what I wanted to do in life, how to treat people, and so many things that I still apply today.

I know how blessed I was to have a father like that, and I see many young men today who didn't have that blessing or those benefits. Probably three out of four young players who come to our team don't know what it's like to have an involved father. We can talk to them about football and they track with us pretty well. But when we talk in the meetings about life issues and character and other things they need to be successful, it's obvious that many of them haven't had that.

Those young men are regular reminders for me of how vitally important fathers are in our society. We can look at many of the other problems we're facing for confirmation of what happens when a dad isn't there: violence in our cities, overpopulated prisons, out-of-wedlock births, and many other consequences. If we don't do something to reverse these trends, our society will likely be in for some real trouble.

In coaching terms, maybe we're in the locker room after a tough first half. My message to all you men on the Championship Fathering team would be, "We've got to stop the momentum against us and then turn it in a better direction and start gaining ground."

You have to start in your own family and nurture your own children. Then, realize that there are many people who are going to grow up without their biological dad. Someone's got to help in that capacity, whether it's a mentor or a relative, a friend, a neighbor, a teacher. We've got to have men like you stepping into the gap.

I believe this book will play a key role in helping us turn the tide, both in our homes and in our society. The research-based outline of loving, coaching, and modeling makes a lot of sense to me. Loving a child and showing him that you care is the most important thing a father can do. If your children don't think you care, then no matter what gifts you give them, no matter how much you're around, you're not going to be able to teach them and have a positive impact on them. But when they know that you really, really care about them, that's when your words and the message you're trying to get across will sink in. Even if they're like I was and they don't necessarily accept everything right away, they'll still be influenced and come back to it.

This can be done in a lot of ways. I'm one of the most old-school people you'll ever meet, but I have a 16-year-old son who likes to communicate by texting. So even though it isn't my thing, I'm learning how to do it, with all the little abbreviations. I'm trying to come into his world a little bit, and that's one way I show him that I care about him.

I can also see many ways in which good coaches and good fathers have similar goals. Both involve teaching and trying to get the best out of individuals, getting them to play up to their potential. Both also aim at getting each person to see that the team is important, that togetherness and unity as a family is what it's all about.

And our modeling is vitally important. Girls need dads to show them how women should be treated by men, so they know what to look for in relationships and will wait for the right type of guy. Boys need to understand who they are as males, to see what it means to grow up in a society and how to be a family man, finding fulfillment in family relationships instead of looking for man-to-man bonding in gangs or other unhealthy places.

I see it on our team all the time, and it's true for fathers as well: People follow the leadership they get, whether it's positive or negative. The leaders of the team or the family will take them in one direction or another. As fathers, it's so important to model responsible living and demonstrate positive, godly manhood for our children.

I learned how to be a father from good models—my father and others. They included men like Clyde Christensen, who has coached on my staff for all the years I've been a head coach. His daughters were a couple of years ahead of mine, so I watched him go through the process and asked him questions. He kept the same schedule I did as a coach—working hard and working long hours—yet he showed me how to be there to nurture my girls and pray for them. He set a great example that I have been able to watch for 13 years so far.

I encourage you to find someone like Clyde—a committed father in a situation much like your own, but a few years ahead of you in the journey. Whether you're a new father, a divorced dad, someone who travels a lot for work, a blended-family father, or whatever, find that other dad and watch him carefully. Ask him questions about his secrets and how he's overcome major challenges. You need those insights and that support.

I believe this book will be a good start for that. You'll learn a lot about fathering from the research of the National Center for Fathering and the stories that Carey Casey shares. You might think of Carey as a more experienced dad who's taking the time to unload some wisdom on you. Soak it all in, and then talk about it with other dads you know.

Carey has been another positive model for my fathering. When I was an assistant coach in Kansas City, we attended the same church and would often get together with our families. I've watched and admired the way he and

Melanie have raised their kids, so I know he has the kind of practical, hands-on wisdom that will help you.

In addition, and probably just as important, I've seen how Carey has placed himself in positions to help others. That's his passion; that's what is on his heart. His life has always been about making a difference for God's kingdom, from his years at Lawndale Community Church in Chicago to his role at the Fellowship of Christian Athletes—and now as CEO at the National Center for Fathering. Carey will tell you that, in his case, CEO stands for "Chief Encouragement Officer," as he is encouraging dads to create a culture of Championship Fathering.

In a day when we often talk about kids who aren't getting proper fathering, I believe it's time to take more of a lead from the guys who are doing it well. We should commend them, but also look at what they're doing and say, "This is what we should strive for. This is the model."

I know Carey is not only saying it when it comes to Championship Fathering; he's done it and he's still doing it. I trust that this book will help you become that kind of father as well.

Introduction

"Boys, let's go for a drive."

I lost count of how many times my father used those words to begin what turned out to be a teaching time. Now that my father is no longer with us, I can't tell you how much I would give to hear those words again.

It took me awhile to catch on. The idea wasn't really about going for a drive. Pop was a lot more subtle than that. He was creating a captive audience in the car, where he could "school us up" on something he'd been thinking about.

He'd slip it into the conversation without making a big announcement. He wouldn't even change his tone of voice. He'd say, "You know, boys, it would break my heart if I ever heard that you hurt a young lady in any way." Or, "If it ever got back to me—and you *know* it would get back to me—that you boys were messing with drugs, we'd have to do some serious business. Know what I mean?"

We would nod our heads. Pop always meant what he said.

I want to be like my dad in many ways, but I don't take my kids out for drives. My young son, Chance, and I walk to the park. I used to take my older kids to fast-food places where we did some fast schooling. Eventually, just like me, they caught on.

What are you hoping your kids will catch on to? Have you repeated certain phrases or habits in an effort to teach father-lessons your kids will remember? If your kids are grown, do you hear them quoting you—maybe to kid you, but also showing they haven't forgotten and that they "got it"? I hope so.

Do you mind if I join you for a while? Let's go for a drive. I'm glad you picked up this book and I hope we connect as you read it.

I have conversations with fathers almost every day. I'm amazed by how much we have in common. It doesn't matter what our backgrounds, racial origins, or careers happen to be. Being dads creates a bond.

We have at least one shared experience: For most of us, fatherhood turned out to be different from the way we thought it would be. Some of the difference was good, and some was not so good. Most of us wish someone had sat us down and schooled us about what it was like to suddenly be Dad.

Some of us had a dad or grandfather who gave us some clues about fathering. But very few of us ever had a conversation that started something like this: "Son, someday you're going to be a father. When that child starts calling you 'Dad,' here's what I want you to remember."

If you did have a conversation like that, I hope you can remember what came next—because it's probably gold! But whatever your preparation for fatherhood, this book can be a series of conversations about the most important aspects of fathering that some of us have learned about along the way. Think of each chapter as you and me taking a drive.

Even though I'm the chief executive officer at the National Center for Fathering, I don't consider myself an expert. But I've got years of practice and access to a lot of help from the National Center. What you'll read in these pages is the result of research and the experiences of many dads including myself. Many of the stories are mine, but the ideas have been tested and proven by generations of fathers.

I realize most men don't take time to read introductions to books, so let me keep this one short.

I don't believe there is a greater challenge a man can take on than the task of being a husband and father. Sooner or later, and more often than you expect, fatherhood will take the best you can give—and then some.

But there's help out there! I've sure needed a lot of it along the way. I trust this book will provide some for you.

Good fathering, even Championship Fathering, is within your reach. It doesn't matter where you're starting as much as it matters how you finish. We've all got a lot to learn. We can learn it from each other's failures and successes. We can help others along the way even while we make progress ourselves.

So let's get started—or let's keep going!

And when someone calls you Daddy, here are some things I want you to remember . . .

—CAREY CASEY
National Center for Fathering
www.fathers.com

CHAPTER ONE

From One Dad to Another

As my co-workers at the National Center for Fathering know, I tend to use illustrations from the world of sports. That's because (1) I'm familiar with athletics, and (2) I know a lot of guys would rather talk sports than talk fathering.

I like to do both.

Until I was seriously injured while playing football for the University of North Carolina, involvement in athletics was a significant part of my life. That allowed me to move into some unusual territory. I was Lawrence Taylor's first roommate in school long before he was a New York Giant or headed for the Hall of Fame. In fact, I was an upperclassman starter when L.T. was wondering if he would make the team!

Later I spent several decades working for the Fellowship of Christian Athletes. And over the years, I've been privileged to be a chapel speaker for every team in the National Football League.

That's why I've been able to count well-known coaches and players among my friends. The picture collection on our refrigerator at home features not only our children but also the families of sports figures with whom we've shared our lives. This might sound glamorous, except that we know these celebrities as people—as mothers, fathers, and children.

One of those people was Reggie White.

A Championship Father

Reggie White played with the Philadelphia Eagles, Green Bay Packers, and Carolina Panthers—and was an ordained minister. Every so often, he'd help me out as a guest speaker. When he visited, he never stayed in a hotel. He always wanted to stay in our home. When I went to visit him, it was the same. At one point, my bride, Melanie, and I had to put a king-sized bed in our guest room for the times when Reggie stayed over.

Reggie White was a giant of a man. But he never considered himself too important to learn more about fatherhood.

Reggie had grown up without positive fathering role models. But he was persistent in trying to find strong father figures by choosing mentors.

I believe that's why he liked staying in our home. I think he wanted to see family. He wanted to see how I as an older guy (maybe six years older) managed my household and raised my kids. He was always searching, seeking to get better beyond football—and fathering was one area in which he was determined to improve.

I was sort of a brother and a father figure to Reggie. He could ask me things, tell me things, share and be honest with me. I was an on-call friend. We didn't talk a whole lot, but when we did the conversations were about things that mattered.

One fatherly trait I observed in Reggie was that he knew how to have fun with our children. When he was with them, he was a big kid. I'm six-one-and-a-half—but I'm also fifty-two years old, so it's tough getting on the floor. This dude was six-five, three hundred and some pounds, and he would hit the carpet with my children, ready for tumbling and wrestling even after he'd played a football game or had a workout. As cool and big-time as he was, Reggie knew how to have fun with kids.

Sadly, Reggie passed away in 2004. And sadly, when I look into the faces of an NFL team today, what I still see most clearly are the effects of fatherlessness.

Some of the faces are those of wealthy young men drifting without dads—and becoming fathers themselves without a clue about what to do next. They're idolized on life-sized posters, but I know they're still little boys, wondering where Dad is and why he doesn't seem to care.

But I also see men like Reggie—young fathers who want to do better than was done for them. They're eager for principles and insights that will help them break the cycle of disappointment from their pasts.

Wherever you are in the fatherhood process, hope begins with what you do as a father from now on. I want you to know what I tell those NFL players: Championship Fathering is a longer-lasting achievement than anything that happens on the field.

Players who've won a championship trophy or ring often declare, "No one can ever take that away from me." That's right. People can't take that away, but they can certainly forget what you've done. The crowd has a short memory, and what it remembers is always selective.

Your kids and grandkids, on the other hand, are in a very special category. They're an audience like no other. When all is said and done, you want them to remember you in the best way—as a Championship Father. That's something worth keeping for eternity.

Are You Championship Material?

I meet men all the time who admit they're defeated by their shortcomings as fathers. They often feel they're simply repeating the failures of their dads. Many bear deep wounds, pain, and resentment toward their fathers. They don't know where to begin to make it right. Maybe that's where you're stuck right now.

There's a lot of practical help in this book, but to begin with I need to give you permission and encouragement to *be* a father. *Start being Dad.*

Your past failures can't erase the biological fact, and your future failures don't mean you can't do your best. You may not even know where your kids *are* right now, but you can accept the truth that you are their father. Begin with that fact; let it sink into your heart.

In these pages we'll look at the patterns of fathering, not the occasional highlight or blooper. Establishing and maintaining a pattern of responsible fathering takes long-term discipline, and it doesn't depend on any single victory or mistake.

I don't know about you, but it's easy for me to think of something good I did as a father and then hang my case on that: "Remember that amazing weekend we went skiing together? That was really fun, wasn't it? Doesn't that prove I'm a good dad?"

That series of questions has a logical answer, though your children may not dare to say it: "Yeah, Dad, that was a great weekend. Where were you the other 51 weekends of the year?"

You and I can't get fatherhood right by doing it well a couple of times, and we can't ruin it with a couple of failures, either. Kids are amazingly forgiving and resilient—more than we deserve!

What *they* deserve from *us* is a pattern of consistency. Our goal is to adjust that pattern into one that gives our children something they need most—a dad committed to Championship Fathering.

He Taught Me Everything I Know

Reggie White wasn't the only Championship Father I've met. When you come right down to it, virtually everything I know about fathering I saw in my dad.

It took me a long time to realize it, but almost every new lesson I learn about fathering I can see illustrated somehow in my dad's life. That doesn't mean I think Ralph Casey was perfect. He made his share of mistakes, but I know I can learn even from those. I have access to a lot more information than he did, but he got things right more often than not.

For example, Pop blended his roles as dad and grandfather in ways that still amaze me. One of our last conversations took place while he lay in his hospital bed as his body and brain were gradually shutting down. He held my hand and looked at me in a way that told me he was still all there. Squeezing my hand and with a twinkle in his eyes and a slur in his speech, he said, "Doooon't provoooke your children to anger!"

As I stood looking down at him, I realized he wasn't just trying to tell me something about my role as a father. He was telling me one of his personal codes of conduct. I thought back over my life as his son, remembering times when I did get angry with him. But it wasn't because he'd provoked me; it was because I knew he was right and wasn't quite ready to agree with him.

One of those times came during high school. I'd been playing football, had experienced some success—and developed a little attitude. I was fortunate to be at a school with a respected football program, but began to think the coach didn't appreciate my abilities as much as he should. I wasn't playing as often as I thought I deserved to play, so I complained.

The coach was a white man, and all my black buddies were telling me to quit the team. We agreed that the way he was treating me must mean he was a racist. My friends said, "Carey, don't play for that white coach. You don't need him."

Their advice sure sounded like the way to go. So I came home, spitting that venom and sharing with my father my plan to quit the team.

Dad listened until I had it all out of my system, then shook his head. "Son," he said thoughtfully, "that man is a good coach. He's going to win football games with or without you. He doesn't need you. You need the team more than the team needs you."

He was right. At that moment I needed someone who could see the bigger picture. That was Pop.

I stayed on the team and played for that coach. Much to my amazement, I improved and he gave me more playing time. Eventually I got a scholarship and played in college—where I met my bride.

Football gave me connections I never could have made otherwise. They all go back to that conversation with Pop; his words literally changed the course of my life. I can only imagine where I'd be today if I hadn't taken his advice. And the older I get, the more quickly I want to agree with him.

My father built into my life the view that learning doesn't stop. Right up until he died, he was pouring wisdom into my mind. He's my greatest example of what Championship Fathering is all about—not just because he was a good dad, but because he taught me that becoming one is all about doing it better and never quitting. If being relentless isn't part of your profile for fatherhood, it's time to add it!

Pop understood the necessity and principles of responsible fathering, even though we didn't use those terms to talk about it. He was practical, down to earth—and experience only helps me understand and appreciate him better.

In preparing this book, I've repeatedly found myself wondering what Pop would say about this or that. I'll mention him often because even when he wasn't perfect (and there were plenty of times when that happened), he remains my best example.

Living the Dream

God must have thought I'd need more than the examples of my dad and Reggie White. He gave me a good dose of equal-opportunity fathering experience, allowing my bride and me to bring four children into the world—two daughters and two sons. He also lets me serve as CEO of the National Center for Fathering, speaking to various audiences about being a dad and meeting with many groups about concerns affecting fathers.

I'm living out my dream. Every time I speak on fathering, I can hear my dad talking about my future and saying I'd be part of a large challenge. Pop planted that dream in me.

Like you, though, I can't forget that my ultimate audience consists of my children. They motivate and evaluate my progress as a dad. They make sure I get plenty of practice. And they help define and refine my purpose as a father.

They know I want to become a better and better father—and grandfather. The arrival of grandchildren has made me aware in a new way of all that comes with the gift of life.

I realize now that my Pop understood what happens when your home is invaded by your first baby grandchild. That little creature creates what a friend of mine calls "happy chaos." When my siblings and I gathered in his home with our families, Pop would sit quietly in the middle of that riot, looking around and smiling. He must have been thinking, *What on earth can I say in all this joy when no one is particularly interested in listening to me at this moment?*

Now I know that his silence was wisdom, for dads and granddads, too. There's a time to speak and a time to be quiet, and Pop knew how to do both. He could be a rock in our family gatherings that the rest of us flowed around, as he said a word here or there or pulled someone aside for a little talk. He was in the center without being the center of attention.

I'm writing, in part, so that my kids will have a better idea what I'm thinking when I'm quietly smiling in the middle of that joyful chaos. I'm writing for my grandchildren and great-grandchildren, too.

And I'm writing for you. So many dads I talk to want to know that Championship Fathering is doable. We won't be perfect at it, but we can get better—a lot better. That's what I'm hoping for you!

Three Little Words

Most of this book is about the three fundamental parts of Championship Fathering: *loving, coaching,* and *modeling.*

The National Center for Fathering didn't pull these three words out of a hat. We interviewed and surveyed thousands of fathers and some children as well, finding that these three areas are crucial. It's a short list, so you and I can remember it. Once you know it, do it, and continuously improve at it, you'll be giving your kids the kind of fathering they need—even when they don't realize it!

Loving, coaching, modeling. As soon as you read those words, you probably had some idea of what I'm talking about. I don't doubt that you could come up with a definition of what it means to love, coach, and model.

But maybe you haven't thought a lot about how those terms apply to *your* role as a father. So I'd like you to put your definitions on hold as you read the rest of this book.

Sure, you'll read some things about loving, coaching, and modeling that will cause you to think, *Yeah that's what I thought,* or even, *That ain't news to me, man!* But I promise you there's more. I can promise that because I've discovered when it comes to fathering, there's always more to learn.

When I first started hanging out with the folks at the National Center for Fathering, I had to put my ideas about being a good dad on hold for a while, too. I had to be schooled in the basics. I had to learn new ways of thinking and look at familiar relationships with new ideas in mind.

All this made me appreciate my upbringing and experiences even more, and in ways I'd never considered. After all, one thing that good research does is to help us see the obvious much better.

This is my desire for you: that your understanding of loving, coaching, and modeling will get a lot wider and deeper than it's ever been before. I want to build on what you already know, using the discoveries of many men who are pulling for you to succeed in your pursuit of Championship Fathering.

Our research continues to confirm that loving, coaching, and modeling are the foundation of understanding and practicing what our children need from us as dads. That's why we'll devote several chapters to these three components. But I need to tell you right off the bat that these three factors don't stand alone, like rock, paper, and scissors. They overlap. Sometimes we can't tell where loving stops and coaching starts. At other times we may think we're being loving but our kids are "reading" us as models. That's why you can patiently explain something to your child (as a wise coach would), assuming that he or she thinks, *Wow, my dad sure knows a lot about the internal combustion engine,* while he or she is really thinking, *Wow, I have no idea what Dad's talking about, but I know he loves me.*

Our job description is loving, coaching, and modeling. None of these parts is optional. We can't just love and skip the coaching or modeling. We're doing better or worse in each of them, all the time.

It may help to picture the three components of Championship Fathering as the individual supports on a three-legged stool. If one leg is missing or too short, the stool will tip. As you read this book, you may discover you haven't been paying much attention to at least one of the "legs." That area will need your special consideration.

Fortunately, overlap can work in your favor, too. A loving dad usually practices coaching and modeling. A dad excels in coaching when he actively loves his kids and is a model for them. And you can't help being an outstanding model when you're loving and coaching.

What You Got, What You'll Give

Championship Fathering is about your legacy, too.

Politicians are asked what kind of legacy they think they'll leave behind, but it usually sounds like a long-term public relations program—a sort of permanent popularity. With this kind of legacy, your family and close friends may be pretty disgusted with your life but everyone else can think you're wonderful! That's not the kind of legacy I have in mind. I'm thinking of one that leaves a deep, meaningful, positive mark on the people who know you best.

Heritage is the legacy you've received. It's not a hot subject today, since it sounds like something you store with antiques in the attic or basement. We live such uprooted lives that it often seems we came from nowhere and no one; we just showed up in our neighborhood one day. People rarely talk about their ancestors, often seeming embarrassed or ignorant or angry about their personal pasts.

I don't know about you, but that's not the kind of heritage I've received or the kind of legacy I want to leave behind. I know I've been blessed with a rich heritage, having been entrusted with my father's reputation and my family's history. As I try to be a good keeper of what I've been given, I need to make sure I expand that heritage and leave a strong legacy for my children.

I recognize the painful fact that a lot of dads don't have the benefits of a positive heritage. But I want to inspire and equip you as a dad to transform whatever heritage you've received into a positive legacy for your children and grandchildren. The past doesn't have to have the last word on the future of your family. You can help reverse the fathering deficit that seems so prevalent in our culture. It's really the best gift you can give your children.

I've gotten to know a number of men whose heritage was nothing short of a handicap. Their fathers and grandfathers didn't seem to care what kind of legacy they were passing on. But I've seen these men take on the challenge of making things different for their own children. I've watched them day by day, patiently taking sad and shameful heritages and creating legacies that would make their children proud and healthy adults. For your kids' sake, don't get so hung up on your heritage that you fail to shape your legacy.

At the National Center for Fathering we often picture legacy-leaving as a huge relay marathon in which each generation is represented by a leg of the race. Each runner passes the baton to the next. The question for each of us is, *What kind of legacy will I pass on to those after me?*

You can't change your heritage, but you can greatly affect the impact of your heritage through the legacy you add to it.

The Job You Can't Avoid

You may be wondering right now if it's worth even trying to be a Championship Father. Your own father may have been such a disappointment that you're reluctant to wear the title of "Dad." Maybe he didn't give you much to work with in developing your own legacy.

Don't give up.

If you have a child, the question isn't whether you're a father. It's how you'll do the job you can't turn down—and whether you'll allow yourself to enjoy it.

Fathers have one unavoidable role: They teach. They teach when they're there, and when they're not. They even teach when they're *never* there.

Fathers teach well or poorly. They coach through what they say and don't say. They model by what they do or don't do. You don't have a choice about teaching; you'll do it one way or the other. But what will you teach?

You'll leave your kids a legacy. You may have been left with little more than pain from those who went before, but that's not what you have to leave your children. You can establish a new tradition. If fatherhood has been given a bad name in your family, you can be the one who makes it a position of honor and dignity. That's a challenge worth a man's best effort!

I don't know the details of what you're facing as a father, and perhaps as a son. But I do know that the core principles of Championship Fathering will give you hope and direction. The fact that you've picked up this book and read this far tells me you have the desire that can turn you into a member of the Championship Fathering team.

The First Day of the Rest of Your Fathering

The National Center for Fathering takes as its mandate words written by an ancient Jewish prophet who predicted what God had in mind for the future:

> He will turn the hearts of the fathers to their children, and the hearts of the children to their fathers. (Malachi 4:6a)

I trust that by the time you're finished with this book, your heart will be turned even more than it is now toward your children.

It's a father's privilege and God-given challenge to take the lead in his kids' lives. It will always be easier for their hearts to turn to you if they know your heart is filled with love for them.

I also trust that you'll decide to become part of the growing movement of Championship Fathering. Today is not too early—nor too late—to start being Dad!

CHAPTER TWO

Championship Fathering: What Is It?

o the words "championship" and "fathering" really belong in the same sentence?

I'm convinced they do. And I'm meeting more and more men who tell me that the goals of Championship Fathering help express who they want to be in the eyes of their children.

But these same men also tell me they don't know where to start. Some of them think they've been "losers" as dads for so long that it's impossible to make up for the opportunities they've lost. They confess that it's hard to think about Championship Fathering because they've had so many "losing seasons."

Maybe you're cringing, expecting to get beaten down by this book. But I won't do that. I've gotten too much help as a dad to think you don't deserve some, too. We're in this together.

The Secret of Championship Fathering

If becoming part of the Championship Fathering team sounds like too high a goal for you, let me tell you the same thing I tell any father who'll listen: Championship Fathering is mostly about time and the basics. You start doing the fundamentals and keep doing them.

Sports champions are teams and individuals who practice and perform their fundamentals better and longer than anyone else. A lot happens in sports that you can't control; but you can control how you do the basics, and that makes all the difference. You can't control everything in fathering, either, but you can do something about the way you pursue the fundamentals.

Before we go further, let's settle on a description of Championship Fathering:

> *Dads involved in Championship Fathering know the fundamentals: loving, coaching, and modeling. They apply those fundamentals to their kids and keep practicing them throughout the seasons of life. These dads also know they're part of a team and make encouraging connections with other team members.*

Loving, coaching, and modeling are so basic to fathering that we'll never outlive learning and practicing them. Doing them for a two-year-old is different from doing them for a teenager. But even when the recipients of our fathering grow up, our basic relationship with them doesn't change. We'll still be Dad. If we live long enough, we can even apply these fundamentals when our kids are grandparents!

Joining the Team

Many of the photographs I have of Pop show him with other men. I have vague memories of hours of conversation in our home and homes we visited—the deep voices, the laughter, the male noises, and the heads nodding in agreement. They left a mark inside me, but I didn't really listen to what those men were talking about. After all, I was busy being a kid.

Now I wish I could go back and listen. When I talk to other men now, I find there are almost always moments when we stop talking and start *relating*. If we spend enough time together, the conversation moves to a deeper level. Usually what we're talking about has something to do with being dads.

Those old pictures of my dad sitting in a lawn chair talking with other men always remind me that fathering may seem like a one-man job, but works best as a team endeavor. I think Pop was the kind of dad he was, in part, because of the kind of friends he had. The men in his life formed a circle of accountability and encouragement.

When it comes to Championship Fathering, I don't just want you to pledge to love, coach, and model on your own. I want you on the Championship Fathering *team*. Even if you've never considered yourself a first-round draft pick before, you're one now! Find other dads who are serious about responsible fatherhood, too. Believe me, they're around. If you're willing to join the team, your seasons of Championship Fathering start today.

Reading this book can be your training camp experience. The skills you already have may need to be sharpened, and you may need to work harder at applying them. But knowing and doing can help you become a Championship Father—one who gives everything he has, every day, to provide his children with the tools they need to lead lives that are emotionally, psychologically, and spiritually rewarding.

Confessions of an Average Dad

My bride, Melanie, and I have been married for more than thirty years now. Our three older children are in their twenties, grown up and married. After a long break we had our fourth child; he's eleven now, and his name is Chance.

People sometimes ask me if we named him Chance because he represents another opportunity to get the parenting thing right. Others wonder if I was just celebrating the chance to be a kid again! Actually, I have a close friend named Chance, and I wanted to honor that relationship.

Anyway, Chance continues to challenge me. He keeps me on my toes, and I need that.

One evening, just a few weeks after I joined the National Center for Fathering, Chance and I were heading up to his bedroom to do our tucking-in ritual. We took a short detour to my study, where he happened to notice a stack of my new business cards. He asked if he could have one.

"Sure, Son," I said.

He read it out loud: "Carey Casey, Chief Executive Officer." Then he read the address and all the numbers, and I could tell he felt proud of his old dad.

Later, in Chance's bedroom, I reached over to turn off the light on his dresser and saw my business card there. On the card, right below my title, in his little chicken-scratch writing, Chance had written these words: *A great father.*

It was a moment I wouldn't trade for anything.

But just in case you think I'm setting myself up as a candidate for Father of the Year, let me tell you about another episode in my relationship with Chance. Seeing his note on my business card had me flying, but before long he brought me back down to earth.

I'd brought home some blank surveys—we call them profiles—from the National Center for Fathering. These questionnaires help dads see how they're doing. We encourage fathers to have their wives and children fill out the profiles, too, and then discuss the results. (See the "Fathering Profile" sidebar.)

I gave one of these forms to Chance. Boy, he went straight to it—really thinking hard about those eight questions. At one point he scratched out his first answer and gave me a lower score. Finally, after what seemed like an hour, he totaled up the points and marked it on the rating scale at the bottom.

How did I score? *Average!*

Chance found that word on the page and circled it, then showed it to me. He rated me pretty highly on most of the questions, but my score was still average compared to those of other fathers who'd taken the profile.

Here I am, CEO of the National Center for Fathering, and I'm an average dad!

I hope that news, which is sobering for me, is a little encouraging to you. All of us face challenges; there are no perfect fathers. Our goal as fathers should not be perfection, but constant improvement.

I consider myself to be a very committed dad. I feel good about the bond

---

FATHERING PROFILE

How do you score in your level of involvement with your child?

1=mostly false   2=somewhat false   3=undecided
4=somewhat true   5=mostly true

1. My child and I often do things together.   Score ____
2. My child accompanies me on errands.   Score ____
3. I frequently read stories to my child.   Score ____
4. I often work together with my child on a project. Score ____
5. My child and I often have fun together.   Score ____
6. My child and I spend a lot of time together.   Score ____
7. I often involve my child in working with me.   Score ____
8. I spend time playing with my child a couple of
   times a week.   Score ____

Total: ____

PLOT YOUR SCORE:

8	16	24	31	36	40
LOW		AVERAGE		HIGH	

Note: The scale is not uniform because it is based on norms from a study group of 1,500 fathers.

I have with Chance, my three other children, and my three "children-in-law"! But I also know there's room for improvement, even at my age. I'm striving to keep learning and growing.

We fathers all fail at times. Sometimes we don't keep promises; we may correct too harshly, or "lose it" over some trivial matter. We may need to give our children more focused attention or just more "hanging out together" time. On a typical day, most of us are just average dads.

Being humbled is a good thing. It reminds us we need help from others, including God. Being humbled can teach us that effective fathering isn't hit or miss, but the result of a plan.

Fortunately, our kids tend to be more forgiving than these fathering profiles. They think we're great even when we're average. Imagine how they feel when they realize we want to be more than average dads!

Listening to the Fatherless

As you seek to be an effective father, you may discover that your kids aren't the only ones who need your attention. Many children don't have a dad involved in their lives. Championship Fathering also means being a father to your own children first—and then extending that love to others.

The other day, Chance and I walked to a neighborhood park together. We chased each other and played tag along the way. It was some great father-son time.

At the park, I planted myself on the bench as Chance ran around trying out the equipment. Pretty soon another boy appeared. He approached me, and soon we shared the bench. His name was Ryan, age 11. We struck up a conversation, and it wasn't long before he and Chance were testing their skills on the monkey bars.

Ryan had a bag with him containing his baseball equipment, and we took turns doing batting practice. The more we got to know this young man, the more he impressed me. He was a very respectful and bright kid.

He lived a few blocks away, he said. He came to the park frequently, on the chance that someone would want to play catch or take a few swings with the bat.

When I asked Ryan about his family, he said, "I don't know my dad." When we parted company, we talked about seeing him again.

As Ryan walked away, I stopped Chance for a quick teachable moment. "Chance, look at Ryan. Who is he with right now?"

"Nobody."

"That's right, Son. And who are you with?"

"I'm with you, Dad."

I talked to Chance about the unfathered kids in our society, many of whom are good kids like Ryan. Chance even said he'd love to have Ryan as his brother.

Sadly, children like Ryan don't have a dad who'll take them to the park. Often they're hungry for someone who'll help them practice playing ball, or show any interest in their lives. Sometimes the male role models available to these kids aren't that great.

I realize I didn't do anything extraordinary that day. But our encounter with Ryan convinced me more than ever that we fathers—we who sense the responsibilities of fatherhood and are highly committed to our families—need to reach out to kids who need us. We can include them in some of our family activities, showing interest and offering a word of encouragement.

As we seek to influence and benefit our own children, God wants to extend that influence. You can begin to do that in some pretty nonthreatening ways—reaching out to your children's friends and neighborhood kids, coaching a sports team, volunteering in youth and children's ministry.

If you haven't heard the voice of the unfathered, let me share what a second-grader wrote for one of our Father of the Year essay contests. This comes from a boy named Dino, asked to write about "What My Father Means to Me." His English isn't perfect, but his message is eloquent:

My dad passed away when I was born. I wish my dad was with my family. I wish my dad was back with me. I miss my dad a lot.

I want to know how my dad looks like. Is a dad bigger than a mom? Is a dad like a grandpa? Is he big? How does a dad look like?

Does he yell at you? Is he mean? Is he nice? Is a dad funny? Does he cook? Does he eat a lot? Does a dad drink beer? Does a dad play basketball?

Is a dad more special than a mom? I just want to know how my dad would be like if he were alive today. I really wish he was with me now.

Kids have a simple, innocent way of putting something charming right next to something heartbreaking. But I think Dino's words capture the emptiness and longing children feel when their dads aren't there.

Dino's father will not hear those words. I wonder if there's a man who'll stand in for that boy's dad. Will someone fill a little of the emptiness in Dino's life?

I also wonder what our sons and daughters would write about us. What would they say a dad looks like? Does he yell? Is he mean? Is he nice? Is he funny? Does a dad play basketball? Does he pray with his kids every day? Does a dad have a twinkle in his eyes?

Our children may or may not sit down to write essays honoring us. But images and words and feelings are being written even today on their hearts.

Dad, what are the words on your child's heart about you? Are there ways in which you've been absent? Are you willing to do what it takes to change that?

The Father's Hall of Fame

I was privileged to attend the NFL Hall of Fame induction ceremony with the family of the late Reggie White, whose friendship I mentioned in the previous chapter. He was perhaps the best defensive lineman ever to play the game—and, as the cliché goes, he was an even better person. In Reggie's case, the cliché was true.

At the ceremony, Reggie's son Jeremy delivered a speech—a moving tribute to his dad. He said, "If life were to have a Hall of Fame for people who were important in society, I would be so bold as to say that my dad would be in the 'Life' Hall of Fame. His passion for God, his love for his family and community, and his dedication to making the world a better place would at least get him nominated."

The people who played with Reggie and knew him agreed with his son. Number 92 could play football, and he was a great husband and dad.

Jeremy White's words about his father describe what I think is a good goal for the rest of us—to be Hall-of-Fame dads. Only those who know us as Dad can vote us into that select group.

So how do we become the kind of dads who belong in the Fathering Hall of Fame? By being teachable.

I vividly remember my dad sitting in his chair—the newspaper in one hand, his Bible in the other. He was always reading and studying; he knew what was going on in the world. He discussed those things with us kids, always with a Bible nearby to give us God's perspective. And he read *with* us.

My dad was always eager to learn and grow; he was teachable. He was a respected leader in the church, though not a pastor. He taught by example that a man could use the Bible as a reliable source of wisdom and a way to hear God speak. It seems that Pop tried not to let a day go by without learning something new and passing something on to his kids.

That's a great way for anyone to approach life, especially dads. Just wanting to improve can make a huge difference.

How else can we grow and be all God wants us to be? We have to be teachable—willing to learn from elders and other dads, from books and speakers, and from people who are different from us.

The ultimate answers, of course, are found in the One who created you and your precious children. Make sure you depend on God—the only perfect Championship Father—for wisdom that has no limits.

When we decide to step up to effective fathering, most of us feel inadequate. God knows better than we do how inadequate we are! Ask Him for specific guidance in every situation or trial.

I'm not kidding here. Get by yourself and talk to God out loud. He's a great listener.

Often when I'm talking to God, I realize what I need to do—or I see something I've been missing. And no subject is out of bounds. You may need to pray about issues with your own dad; maybe there's a destructive habit holding you back as a father. Perhaps your son or daughter faces a challenge, or you have a continuing disagreement with a child. God is the source of all wisdom, and He's promised to be there when you call to Him.

A teachable dad is willing and eager to learn and grow. That's one of the marks of flexibility. So is being humble enough to go to God and ask for help.

Aiming High

A growing number of dads are waking up to the joys of fatherhood. More and more influential business leaders and politicians are talking about their families as a priority.

But many of these dads don't make headlines. They simply have an experience that awakens their "father hearts," and they decide to invest more of themselves in their families. The world may not be watching, but I can tell you those fathers' kids are paying attention.

The choices aren't always easy. They may involve walking away from career opportunities that might boost your sense of status and worth. But that can't compare to the rewards of building strong connections with your children. Knowing you've been there for your kids is an achievement you can cherish.

In the end, it doesn't matter what title is on your business card. A more important legacy is your relationship with your children, and how *they* describe what you do in life.

The point of pursuing Championship Fathering isn't to get some kind of glory or recognition. It's to have a powerful, positive impact on your children's lives.

Championship Fathers want to be difference-makers. They want to know that they met one of the most basic challenges in life—the challenge of fatherhood.

CHAPTER THREE

—

Getting Involved
with Your Kids

F ootball was my main sport when I was growing up. But during my
freshman year in high school, I joined the wrestling team.

The fact that I was able to beat the other two guys in my weight class
shows how badly they needed me. I had no experience, but had heard from
other football players that wrestling would help keep me in shape if I wasn't
going to play basketball during the winter.

One day there was an all-school assembly so that everyone could watch
us wrestle. As we were getting ready, my dad entered the gym! He'd left work
so he could watch me. That may not sound like a big deal today, but back
then dads just didn't do that.

Pop was involved. He came to support me. Unfortunately, on that day
I was pinned in about a minute and twenty seconds. I remember being on
my back and looking up at the lights—something I must have done at least
four times before I ever won a match.

Wrestling was not my calling; it was not fun. But my dad was there for
every match. He encouraged me and let me know he knew I was trying, even
though I was losing. He was pleased with my effort, and that kept me going.

After I told that story recently, a mom and dad described to me their 23-
year-old twin boys who play tennis doubles. Even as young adults, those sons

keep glancing at the bleachers during matches to see their dad. They always know where he's sitting. His support gives them great confidence.

I know you're busy, and it's hard to attend all your kids' events throughout the year. But children long to look out and see their daddy watching them perform and compete—win or lose. Sometimes it may seem like you're sitting in those bleachers for days at a time, but in the end you'll find that those days have gone by so quickly.

I'm not saying that the choice of whether to attend your child's event during working hours is an easy one. Many of us, due to the nature of our jobs, don't have the flexibility to leave work for a couple of hours. But if you do have that option, I hope you'll consider it. Don't promise to be there if you're not sure you can make it, though; better to show up unexpectedly than to make excuses afterward.

When it comes to involvement, nobody can take your place. And involvement starts with being there. If you don't spend any time in your kids' world, the wisdom you have to share with them may not get a hearing.

The Involvement Investment

Loving, coaching, and *modeling*—the basics of Championship Fathering— have something in common. They all require *involvement.*

Being involved will take unique shape in your family. But there are some principles every dad can apply.

Remember all those books and articles and TV shows about parenting that emphasized the importance of "quality time" with kids? The idea was that children didn't really benefit from spending time with us unless it was quality time—no matter how much "quantity time" we spent. The discussion usually boiled down to doing something "high quality" with a child in 10 minutes so you didn't have to waste a whole hour accomplishing little.

The real waste was the discussion. I wonder if anyone asked a child, "Do you know the difference between quantity time and quality time with your dad?" I'm sure the answer would have been, "Huh?" and the discussion would have been over.

Children can't distinguish between quality time and quantity time. Most adults can't, either. What we do know is that when there's a limited *quantity* of time, there's not likely to be much *quality* time.

Today we talk about the differences between "investing time" and "spending time." Maybe that's just the same discussion with different terminology. But I think there's something to be said for keeping our schedules flexible enough that we can enjoy unstructured, kid-planned time as well as parent-planned time designed to achieve certain goals.

I know one dad who created an agenda for himself when he was thinking about a conversation he wanted to have with his son. He even handed those little slips of paper over during their talks. That boy treasures those little written agendas as reminders of his dad's involvement in his life.

There's nothing wrong with saying that we "spend" time with our kids (or standing in line at the store). But as we manage our schedules and make time for our families, we need to think of time as something we *invest,* not something we just *spend.*

If you put your money in an IRA or stocks or real estate, it's still yours—and, hopefully, growing. It's invested to help you reach a particular goal. Even when you've *spent* money by trading it for electricity or a big-screen TV, you're investing. Some investments bring valuable, long-term dividends; others are more like tossing a fistful of cash into the wind.

Funds, of course, are limited. If you're investing money in one place, you've chosen *not* to invest it in another.

Time is the same way. We choose how to invest every minute, and our children are clearly one of the highest-yield investments.

Since time, like money, is a limited resource, budgeting is vital. We have to prioritize. Much of our time goes toward providing for our families, and that's important. But if it takes us away from family, it's like piling up debt. Do you need to make some changes in your "time portfolio"?

Financial experts also say it's important to focus less on the *price* of an investment and more on the *value* you're receiving. Is the mountain-climbing trip or the new model-rocket-launching hobby worth the time? What if it's a great opportunity to bond with your son or daughter?

This isn't an argument to invest only in "quality" activities you think will be the most rewarding. That's a high-risk proposition with little promise of long-term success. It's the steady, smaller investments of quantity time that yield the best results over the years.

Here's an example—something the Casey family does that may work for yours, too.

We take walks together. Long walks, short walks, city walks, forest walks.

There are great benefits. It's good to get away from the TV, the computer, the "to do" list, whatever keeps us from connecting. It's like taking a mini-vacation—getting out in God's creation, letting go of tension, discovering new perspectives. If the kids are getting on each other's nerves, a walk gives them something new to think about. It's a natural time to enjoy each other.

It's also a purposeful time. Walking together provides opportunities to touch base, catch up on the events of the day, ask questions, make plans, share dreams, laugh together. And if everyone agrees to leave his or her electronic gadgets at home, there's little chance of interruption.

It's even a time to connect with our neighbors. Instead of just waving as we open our garage door and disappearing inside our house, we stop and get to know other families. Often we discover neighbors who need help with a project or a word of encouragement.

We don't worry about figuring out whether we just experienced quantity or quality time. You don't have to, either. Just aim at spending time together!

That doesn't mean just being in the same room, by the way. Surfing the Internet on separate laptops three feet apart isn't quantity *or* quality time. Spending (or investing) time means *being* together, whether you're planning the next family adventure or building a snowman.

Time with our children has the potential to pay huge dividends. As folks at the Young Life youth ministry used to say, we want to be "wasting time with kids." Only God knows the difference that will make for our children, grandchildren, and great-grandchildren.

Don't Leave Involvement to Mom

Some dads seem to think that being involved in a child's life is "the mother's job." Diaper-changing, doctor visits, parent-teacher conferences, brother-sister battles—anything that requires "dealing with the kids"—is seen as female territory.

One father I know reversed this trend in his household. After struggling with a particular annoyance during family vacations, he stepped up to fix it instead of leaving it to his wife.

The problem was all those stops for gas. He called them "junk food and useless stuff gauntlets." He dreaded stopping for fuel because he knew he'd be bombarded with requests for overpriced toys and unhealthy treats. Those episodes made him irritable, so he came up with a plan of action.

Once family members planned a trip, Dad counted how many days they'd be on the road. Then he went out and bought inexpensive but special treats, games, books, and surprises while he was still at home. After labeling a brown paper bag for each day and filling it with his purchases, he packed everything in the car.

Before the family left home, this dad gave his children the following instructions: "There's a bag for each day, and it will be opened first thing in the morning after everyone is packed up and we're ready to hit the road. In the bag is enough to last us for the whole day—trust me. In return, you will not bother to ask me for anything when we stop for gas along the way."

The kids were excited. They enjoyed discovering and sharing the contents of the bags. For the first time, getting going in the morning wasn't a problem. Neither were gas station "gauntlets."

That dad could have kept grumbling and pressed his wife to "deal with the kids." But he took a proactive, creative approach to the problem—and ended up having a great time on vacation. Getting involved does have its rewards.

Two-Way Involvement

Not long ago, I was tucking young Chance into bed. After I gave him a hug and a kiss, he said, "Dad, would you lay down with me?"

"What did you say, Son?"

"Can you lay down next to me, Dad?"

"Okay, for a minute," I said. I wasn't sure whether this was a ploy to stay up later or an opportunity for time together.

"Here, Dad," he said, pulling back the covers. "You get under here, too."

So I did. We lay there for a while, talking.

Finally Chance said, "Tell me about Rev, Dad." Rev was short for Reverend—a golden retriever we'd had before Chance was born. Rev's father was Bishop, and *his* father was Deacon. Chance loves to hear stories about Rev, maybe because it's part of our family history.

So I told him about Rev. We had such a good time, in fact, that I got a little reckless. I snuck downstairs for some wheat crackers, brought them back, and we ate them in the bed as we talked—even though Chance had already brushed his teeth!

It was one of those father-child times of connection that sneak up on you and make you thank God for your children all over again. It may not happen every night or even once a week—but when it does, you don't want to miss it!

It was also a reminder that my son wants to know about me and my world. He wants to share my space, know what my cheek feels like, what I smell like, what I did when I was his age—even what excuses I tried in order to stay up a little later.

Often when I talk about involvement, dads think I'm just telling them to participate in their children's events. But involvement goes both ways. Your kids want to be part of *your* life, too.

While you're spending time in their world, make sure you let them spend time in yours. Letting your kids into your life is a key to being part of theirs.

Involvement That Stretches

One summer, Melanie and I let Chance talk us into an afternoon at a local water park. I have to admit it was not the first thing I thought of doing when I woke up that morning.

I kept thinking things like, *I'm past 50 now! I'm too old for this. These places are for dads who are 20 years younger than I am.* What would they say in the emergency room when I showed up in my swimming trunks with a broken neck?

One of the main features of the park was a huge water slide. That's where Chance and I headed first, of course. It just seemed like the manly thing to do.

We hiked up the long stairs. At the top was a sign that said, "If you have problems with your heart, you might not want to ride this monster"—or words to that effect. But no worries; the lifeguard showed me the proper sliding technique, and I tamed that monster. Chance came down right behind me, smiling all the way!

Chance was in awe—an old man going down a water slide! But hey, I'm a dad; isn't that what dads do? I may have started the day with doubts, but by the time we'd tried most of what the park had to offer, I knew this was the place I most wanted to be, with my son.

Sure, there's a middle-aged guy staring back at me in the mirror, but I can't think about that. My focus is on what my son needs me to do. I can't sit there, saying, "Okay, Son, you go climb that thing, and I'll wait down here." I didn't do that with Marcellus, Christie, and Patrice, my older kids. If at all possible, I want to be that kind of dad with Chance.

I even want to have some gas left in the tank for an active life with my grandchildren. I've got a friend my age who's rock climbing and snowshoeing with his grandkids. Now that's involvement!

We fathers all have areas where we need to stretch a little. Maybe you have a daughter, and relating to her on her terms doesn't come naturally to you. Maybe you never played soccer in your life, but your child's team needs a coach. Maybe your child shows an interest in chess, and you don't know checkmates from checkers. Maybe the family you grew up in didn't show a lot of affection, but your children need hugs.

Moving boldly out of our comfort zones is what dads need to do! It may take a crash course in soccer or chess, but you can handle that. Many dads do the same thing I did at that water park—seeing a chance to connect with their children, they don't hesitate.

So go for it—or keep up the good work. Involvement isn't just being a spectator at your kids' events; real involvement means you participate whenever possible.

Involvement That Intervenes

Getting involved with your kids sometimes means intervening to protect them. A lot of people will try to influence your children, and many of them may get your endorsement. But at other times you'll need to step in to keep your kids safe.

Did anyone ever offer you something attractive but suspicious? That happened to me, and I'm thankful my Pop was there to reel me in.

During my last year of high school, I received attention from some university football programs. If you've heard shady things about athlete recruiting today, I'd say it was worse back then.

I knew some big colleges were looking at me, but I hadn't worked hard enough in class to qualify academically. Still, at a year-end banquet an assistant coach from a major university came over to talk to me. He said, "Carey, don't worry about it. We got it all under control; you're in school."

I knew I didn't qualify, but liked what he was telling me. "Sounds great!" I said.

I thought my dad was off somewhere else, but he was right behind me. "No," he declared. "He didn't qualify." Then he added, "No, Carey's going to prep school or junior college."

Desperately I thought, *Quiet, Dad! Didn't you hear the man? I can go and play Division I my freshman year; I can be playing on TV!* But my dad saw through all that, and intervened.

I ended up going to junior college in a small town—and had a great experience. I did well on the football field, but mostly I grew up as a person. I developed good study habits and disciplines I'd never picked up in high school—and probably wouldn't have developed at a big university. And I became a leader on campus.

If my daddy hadn't stood up for what was right, I would have gone straight to a four-year college without qualifying. I could have cheated and played football there. But chances are I would have flunked out and never would have gone anywhere.

I can see how my dad protected me from those dangers; he really protected me from myself. He stepped in and kept me on a pathway that was best for me.

Maybe you have a similar story. Experiences like that drive home the fact that young people can go down the wrong path when they don't have a father or father figure looking out for their best interests—and who are willing to intervene. Kids still need our guidance when they're teens and young adults. That takes involvement.

Championship Checklist

Research by the National Center for Fathering has helped us find ways to measure how involved dads are in their children's lives. If you want to see how you're doing in this area, here are seven statements to consider. How well do they apply to you?

1. *I often discuss things with my child.* Even before your child can understand, get used to talking to him or her in a conversational tone. You may discover your toddler will sit in rapt fascination as you describe the details of your work or the intricacies of the zone defense. The point is to help your child grow up thinking, *Dad has always talked to me about stuff.*

Be patient when your kids ask questions. When they're very young, that may be all they seem to do! At that age they actually think you know all the answers, and you may be tempted to fool them as long as you can. But sometimes kids need to hear you say, "That's a good question. I have no idea what the answer is!" Find out together.

2. *My child and I often do things together.* Get comfortable in your kids' world and welcome them into yours. Teach your child early the concept of riding along with Dad. Be on the lookout for projects you can do together, or simple parts of larger tasks that a child can do with you. Play the time-honored game called "Hand Daddy the Tool."

3. *I schedule time to spend with my child.* Too often, family time isn't protected against time requests from others. But you can "make appointments" on your schedule with each of your kids and your wife. If someone wants to claim that time, simply say, "I've already got an appointment then that I can't break." Every family needs some time that's protected by a firewall.

4. *I teach my child skills.* Who taught you to ride a bike or shoot a basketball? What about flying a kite, changing a tire, driving a stick shift? Make a list of skills you learned as you grew up and decide which ones you'll pass on to your kids. Spread these out over time and keep them age-appropriate. Don't forget to be patient, too.

5. *I take an active role in my child's education.* Being married to a teacher, I can tell you that most dads could be much more involved in their children's education. Do you know the teachers, coaches, and administrators who have the biggest impact on your child?

Meet them. Compare notes with your wife. It makes a good impression when both parents visit with the teacher. When the news is bad, they can share the load; when it's good, they can share the glow.

6. *I am involved in my child's life.* This seems like a no-brainer, but for too many dads it's a no-clue.

Can you name your child's three closest friends? Where would you start looking if she was suddenly missing? What's his favorite ice cream? When your child dreams of being grown up, what career does he or she have?

We need to continuously update our mental profiles of each of our children. We want our children to think, *My dad really knows me.*

7. *My child and I often have fun together.* When our children are very young, we usually figure out what makes them laugh. A ticklefest, for instance, may send them (and us) into gales of laughter.

Do everything in your power to keep the laughter and fun in your relationship with your kids. Watch for activities that you and your child like—and enjoy them often. If you don't know yet what you both like, experiment. At the very least, find out what your kids love to do and join them in the fun.

Don't Miss the Joy of Involvement

When I first came to the National Center, I heard all about WATCH D.O.G.S.® (the "D.O.G.S." stands for "Dads Of Great Students"). It's our safe school initiative, getting fathers and father figures involved to help create a more secure learning environment. Not long ago I finally had a chance to spend a day at Chance's school as a WatchDOG.

When I walked in, they handed me an itemized schedule for the day. I got a set of keys with instructions to lock certain doors, and a walkie-talkie with directions on what to look for and whom to call if anything happened. My agenda included time in five classrooms, lunch and recess with Chance, patrolling hallways, and regularly scanning the parking lot, playground, buildings, and perimeter.

I helped kids with reading. One little girl came up to me and said proudly, "I'm on my third book."

On the playground, the boys asked me, "Can you be our quarterback?" The girls wanted to know, "Could you watch us play?"

I spent a few minutes working on math flash cards with a girl. When we were done, she asked, "Can I come back and do it again?"

I saw a sense of accomplishment when kids learned something new. Plus, I got a very needed refresher course on state capitals!

That day really changed my perspective. I'd met with national leaders on Capitol Hill and with the Kansas City Chiefs, but when I put on a WATCH D.O.G.S. shirt my status seemed to rise to a whole new level—at least with those kids. I made a deeper connection with my own son and with many of the others in his school.

When the day was over, I couldn't believe how quickly it had gone. I'd learned so much, and had even made a difference.

Involvement does that for you—and for the kids in your life. You can find out more about WATCH D.O.G.S. at www.fathers.com/watchdogs. But whether or not you get involved in that particular program, please be involved with your children.

We live in times that seem to conspire against involvement with our kids. Divorce and work expectations are just two factors that sap time and energy to the point that involvement can seem like an endurance test.

It doesn't have to be that way. Just as I discovered the joys of flash cards and watching kids play at Chance's school, you can discover the joys that involvement brings to members of the Championship Fathering team.

 ACTION POINTS

How to Stay Involved

Preschool
- Go on a walk with your child and collect leaves or other objects that reflect the changing seasons.
- Create habits that help you connect with your wife and kids, such as phone calls from work or special "daddy" time when you walk through the doorway at the end of the day.

- Post pictures of your children where you'll see them on the way home from work (on your car dashboard, for example). As you look at the pictures, tell yourself, "The next few hours are the most important in my entire day."
- Tell your child a funny story, using voices, motions, facial expressions, and sound effects to make it come alive.
- What causes laughter and silliness in your daughter? What brings that mischievous grin to your son's face? Find out, and then capitalize on it for the benefit of your relationship.
- Get on your child's level—squatting, on your knees, or lying on the floor—when talking to or playing with him or her.
- Carve out a few hours when you can give your child focused attention, doing nothing other than getting to know him or her better.
- Read a book with your child, asking lots of questions as you go.
- Be the one to jump up and help when your child has a need. Those are priceless opportunities—and Mom probably could use a break!

Elementary
- Clear some time this weekend and ask your child, "What would you like to do together?"
- At your kids' sports events, make it your goal to be conspicuously and contagiously positive. Set the tone with lots of encouragement and fun.
- Regularly walk or drive your child to or from school.
- Bring home a funny joke or stunt that you can enjoy with your children.
- Ask what skill your child would like to learn in the next year, then commit yourself to help him or her in that area.
- Go for a drive with your child, just to get away and spend time together.
- Do something special for milestone events in your child's life, such as birthday number 10.

- Be involved in your child's education—including helping with homework, practicing for sports or other activities, and attending school meetings and events.
- Volunteer for a day or half-day at your child's school—perhaps through the WATCH D.O.G.S. program.
- Start regular one-on-one outings with your son, or daddy-daughter dates.

Teen
- Commit to a vigorous outdoor activity over the weekend with your kids. Push the limits and be creative.
- Listen to music that your child enjoys—keeping an open mind.
- Keep "dating" your daughter and scheduling fun activities with your son on a regular basis.
- Figure out how to have fun with your teen by immersing yourself in his world for an afternoon. Hang out together, read a book she likes, play his games, listen to her stories, etc.
- Connect with other adults who play an important role in your child's life—coaches, teachers, youth leaders—and compare notes on how your child is progressing.
- Shock your son or daughter by doing something together on his or her "turf"—skateboarding, hoops at the playground, going to the mall.
- Plan special "rite of passage" events when your children reach milestone ages like 13, 16, and 18.
- Tell your child you'll pay if he goes to a movie with you. Afterward, ask questions about the film's themes.

For additional practical tips on fathering, subscribe to the National Center for Fathering's free e-mail, *fathers.com weekly*, at www.fathers .com/weekly. You'll also find articles on a wide range of fathering situations and challenges at www.fathers.com.

CHAPTER FOUR

Love 101

I know you must be shocked that the CEO of the National Center for Fathering is not the ideal father. In fact, if you're anything like me, you sometimes think, *Man, I'm terrible! I'm a pitiful dad.*

Those thoughts especially used to creep up on me Sunday mornings, on the way to church. You know how sometimes we're rude to our bride or we holler at the kids because they're making us late, or we're swinging our arm in the backseat trying to get them settled down? It's a miserable ride—but we're all going to church!

We're all angry and arrogant, but when we go into the church building there's a sudden miracle. "God bless you," we tell everybody. "How are you doing, Sister Smith? I hope things are going well with you, Brother Bob. Oh, I see they have communion trays set up in the sanctuary. We must be having communion today. Shall we now?"

After the sermon we repeat the "nice routine" on the way out. But as soon as we get back in the car, out it comes again:

"You better put that seat belt on *now!*"

"Everybody quiet down!"

"No, we're *not* going to McDonald's!"

We pick up right where we left off when we parked earlier. It's like we put part of us "on pause" and then hit "play" again. What's displayed isn't pretty.

So how can I talk about the first ingredient of Championship Fathering—

loving? And how can you stand to listen, knowing that you probably don't measure up, either?

We can never love perfectly in this life, but we can be more conscious of what we're doing and adopt a position of humility. When we fail, we must admit it, confess it, and ask for forgiveness. When we try to pose as Super-dad we may think we're fooling our kids, but we're not. They see right through to our faults and weaknesses.

We can commit to improve. We may need to seek accountability from other dads, help from our children's mother, even counseling. It all starts with realizing that even in our imperfections, we can be a living example of hum-ble dependence on our heavenly Father, the ultimate role model.

God loves us and shows us how to love. And there's no arena in which it's more crucial to practice this lesson than the one we call home.

Firm, Flexible Love

I wear two rings on my body every day.

One is a golden band that reminds me constantly of the promises I made to my bride. Before I slipped that ring on her finger and she slipped one on mine, we promised to love and cherish one another.

The other ring is a blue rubber wristband—available at fathers.com—inscribed with those three little words: *Loving, Coaching,* and *Modeling.*

My wedding ring is valuable and unchanging. The vows I made the day Melanie and I became husband and wife were intended to be precious and enduring—like gold.

The rubber ring on my wrist represents my promises to my children and the special aspects of our relationship. The material it's made of reminds me that I can expect to be stretched by my kids. It drives home the point that being a dad is a call to be flexible. If I'm *inflexible* and my children stretch me (because that's what children do whether they want to or not), then some-thing's got to give—and not in a good way!

Being a loving father is a demanding balance between firmness and flexibility. My kids (and my bride) need to know that there are some solid, unchanging things about me—the core of who I am as a man, husband, and dad. They also need to know that I can flex with life; that I'm learning, too; and that even though I haven't got everything figured out, I'm on my way.

One thing my wedding ring and the wristband share in common: Neither will break. I want my kids to understand that. It shapes the way in which my family experiences love from me.

Love: The Fundamentals

When we see X's and O's, many of us men imagine a coach kneeling in front of a bench full of athletes, or standing in front of a chalkboard. He's drawing out the next play or making an adjustment in the defense or offense, adding, "They're killing us out there!"

But did you ever get a note or card from a young lady when you were growing up that was signed with X's and O's?

Does your wife still send you messages that end with X's and O's?

Have you ever used your fingertip to write X's and O's on your bride's forearm when you were driving or just sitting together? (If you haven't, try it.)

In sports, X's and O's stand for the fundamentals. In life, they stand for hugs and kisses—and love in general.

When it comes to Championship Fathering, love *is* fundamental. We have to start with loving.

But wouldn't you know it—love is a tough one for us men. I mean, most of the time, many of us feel clueless! Is loving a man thing? If it is, how do we do it?

Most of us men have a lot more questions than answers when it comes to love. Whether it's loving as husbands or as fathers, we tend to think it's going to be too hard to figure out. So we give up.

Let's start with love—the idea, the attitude, the action. It's the most basic of the basics. That's why it's worth figuring out.

Looking for Love

Most of the men I spend time with have a real problem with the word *love*. It goes way beyond the fact that we overuse the term to describe all sorts of relationships and situations.

For one thing, many men think *love* is another word for *sex*. Or they think it's about feelings.

Most of us probably know that love is about more than sex. But the feeling thing is a mystery for us.

Let's say you turn to your wife while the two of you are taking a walk and say, "I love you." You just suddenly thought it would be a good thing to say.

But then she asks, "What are you feeling right now?" You may have a hard time coming up with an answer.

I don't think the problem is that men don't have feelings. We're just not used to identifying them or talking about them. When we hear our child say "Daddy" for the first time, we can't describe the emotions that little word creates.

This affects relationships. For example, do you, as a man, hesitate to say, "I love God"? Does it seem awkward?

How easily does the following roll off your tongue? "You know Frank, Joe, and Rashid, my neighbors down the street? I love those guys!"

The awkwardness of "man love" gets used in humor all the time. Remember the advertisements that used the punch line, "I love you, man!"? When we men say "I love you" to anyone, we hope we won't get asked, "So, what are you feeling right now?"

If that's not awkward enough, ask yourself whether you feel "loving" toward those who don't feel the same way about you. Jesus talked about the necessity of loving our enemies—a subject most of us don't even want to go near! He even told us to "do good to those who hate you" (Luke 6:27). But retaliating with kindness doesn't seem to be enough.

No, love isn't just about sex or even emotions. In fact, we don't have to talk seriously about love for very long before it starts to look complicated.

The Look of Love

When it comes to understanding the meaning and importance of loving, I have to rely on more than my own observations and experiences. So I go right to the source.

God, the Bible tells me, is love. And God's Son, Jesus, had some amazing things to say about love that make more and more sense to me the longer I try to put them into practice.

One day Jesus was asked what was the most important commandment (Mark 12:28). Here's His response:

> "The most important one," answered Jesus, "is this: 'Hear, O Israel,
> the Lord our God, the Lord is one. Love the Lord your God with all
> your heart and with all your soul and with all your mind and with all
> your strength.' The second is this: 'Love your neighbor as yourself.'
> There is no commandment greater than these." (Mark 12:29-31)

I believe the Great Commandment is the key to grasping the *loving* part of Championship Fathering. Love isn't nearly as much about how you feel as it is about what you *do* for the other person and how you make *him or her* feel. In other words, you don't have to start feeling in order to start loving.

As a friend of mine pointed out, loving is responsible and deliberate beneficial action on behalf of another. Doing good to or for someone is loving that person. Seeing a need or recognizing where you can help is part of showing love.

Love is making wise and practical decisions for the good of another without regard to our feelings. Life is so complex and exhausting that your expressions of love will sometimes simply have to be an act of your will. You can practice love when you don't feel a thing!

The Great Commandment talks about showing love in four ways: heart, soul, mind, and strength. There's a lot there that isn't about feelings! Yes, there's heart, which we usually connect with emotion. But there's also soul, which I think means expressing loving actions and thoughts from the core—whether or not we feel anything at all.

Soul-love is figuring out the loving thing and doing it, no matter what we're feeling at the time. We can love God that way, just plain deciding to trust Him with our lives. We can love our kids that way, too. That includes times when we're inclined to do otherwise—like sucking it up and being patient with a child who's driving you up the wall!

Loving with the mind is definitely a man thing—thinking through the challenge of love, deciding to do what's right regardless of how the other person has treated you, finding out what would be meaningful and helpful to your loved ones. We use our minds to observe our children and act on those observations. In a sense, you're loving your kids by reading this book!

And strength—what man isn't instinctively challenged to express care and value by using his physical abilities to lift, carry, work, and protect? Since we can't turn feelings off or on, why not concentrate on what we can control—putting our wills, minds, and backs into doing for others what will make them feel loved?

Where Love Comes From

But where does the love come from that you use to love God, your neighbor, yourself—and your kids?

Does it start with us? No.

We're not the source of love. We can't love better than we've been loved. Whenever we love, we're giving back or passing on something that was given to us. If we haven't been loved or don't know we've been loved, we'll have to discover love ourselves before we can offer it to someone else—even God.

If we don't understand this, our efforts to love our wife and children are going to fall short. Learning this can and should happen long before we're married and have kids—though often it doesn't.

We can't give what we haven't received. Are you hearing me? We can't love unless we've been loved.

This cuts right to a man's heart. Many of us were raised by dads who had a hard time showing love because *they* were raised by dads who were equally in the dark.

It's a vicious circle. If your dad really loved you and showed you as much, you understand how important receiving love is before you try to pass it on. I can pretty much guarantee that you're going to father as you've been fathered, unless you intentionally choose another path and get any necessary help. You're going to love as you've been loved.

This is why it's crucial for each of us to connect with God's love. The Great Commandment to love God and neighbor was given by the One who is love.

God is the original, inexhaustible source of love. Even the most loving father can't love his family more than God does. The greatest gift a dad can give to his children is to love them and connect them with their heavenly Father, the ultimate source of love.

If You Didn't Get Love

Several years ago I started using a method of passing on some of the love I'd been fortunate to receive. When I'm with a person who didn't have a good relationship with his father and who expresses some deep concern or need, I may pull him aside for a few minutes to talk. This is what I say, and I hope that if you have a broken or painful relationship with your dad, you'll hear these words, too:

> I was blessed to have a great dad. But I'm sure that if your dad could do it over again, and he had the information and the opportunities that he needed, he would be different. There are things in place now that weren't in place then, so your dad didn't give you that. I'm not your dad, but let me say what I believe your dad would say if he were here: *"I'm proud of you."*

Often, men will break down and cry right there—even football players whose arms are bigger than my legs. They weep because I've helped them address a gap in their lives. They just needed to hear those words: "I'm proud of you." Until they heard that phrase, many didn't know what was missing.

Time after time I've had men say to me, "You know, I honestly think my dad loved me, but he couldn't seem to say the words. I thought he was proud of me, and there were times when I could see it in his face, but he never told me."

You're never too old to hear your father say, "I love you. I'm proud of you." And you're never too old to start saying it to your kids and grandkids.

Just because you've never done it, or you think saying the words will be hard, or you're afraid you might break down as you're saying them—none of that lets you off the hook. Those you love need to know without a doubt that you love them.

I hope you'll find the strength to forgive your father for his shortcomings in loving you and receive the loving, proud blessing of your heavenly Father. Let it sink into your own life—and pass it on to your children and grandchildren.

The Best Father of All

"I love you. I'm proud of you."

That blessing comes from the story of Jesus' baptism in Matthew 3:13-17.

When His closest followers asked Jesus to teach them to pray, He told them to begin their prayers with a phrase we're so familiar with we don't stop to think about it often enough—"Our Father in heaven" (Matthew 6:9). Next time you pray the Lord's Prayer, realize that you're starting by calling God "Dad."

After Jesus was baptized, He received an audible blessing from His Father: "This is my Son, whom I love; with him I am well pleased" (Matthew 3:17). God, the perfect Father, knew that Jesus would benefit from that encouragement. The Father affirmed Jesus as a loved Son of whom He was proud.

It's pretty obvious that all of us need that kind of affirmation from our earthly fathers as well. I'm fortunate to know that my father loved me and was proud of me. And I never got tired of hearing it.

That's why, in our fathering seminars, we often ask fathers to stand up if their dads left them a difficult heritage. Then we have other dads lay hands on them as we adapt that blessing from God: "You are My son, whom I love. In you I am well pleased." It's a very healing exercise for those men.

Get on Board the Love Train

You may be thinking, *All right, Carey. I know I need to love better. But I need some places to start, some hints. I may need even more than hints, 'cause I'm afraid I still don't really get it.*

That's what we're going to do in the next two chapters. We'll take a hard look at two kinds of people Jesus had in mind when He said, "Love your neighbor as yourself"—wives and children. If we can learn to love them, along with loving God, we'll make big strides toward being on the Championship Fathering team.

CHAPTER FIVE

How to Love Your Children

C oming on board at the National Center for Fathering involved a large dose of learning. Some people may think fathering is supposed to "just happen," but I've been encouraged to find that it's a learned skill.

That means I can learn it, and so can you! True, you won't get up one morning and say, "I'm finally a great dad, and I've got nothing else to prove or improve." Fathering is too full of surprises for that. But you can learn— even about something as "automatic" as how to love your children.

How Deep Is Your Love?

A friend of mine told me about a young military veteran whose firstborn was a son. No father was prouder or more eager to raise that boy the right way.

But when his bride became pregnant with their second child, the two of them discovered during an ultrasound that they would soon be parents to a little girl.

The veteran approached my friend with two big questions:

"Can I love two kids as much as I love one child?"

"Having a boy seemed so natural; what do I do with these feelings that I'm not sure I want to have a daughter?"

Ever had questions like those?

It's easy to think of love as a container of feelings that can run dry if we give too much away. One child, we assume, can get maximum love; two children have to share that amount equally.

Is it true that the more kids you have, the less love each will get? Do we have only so much love to give away? Or do we find that love expands *as* we give it away?

I believe the latter is the case. I've also found that the more aware I am of how much I've been loved and am being loved, the easier it is to love.

My bride and I have four children, and each gets maximum love. I've been amazed how my capacity to love has grown now that three of my children are married and I have even more "kids" to love. Now that my grandchildren are arriving, I've got this love thing on a roll—so bring on more grandkids!

That young veteran had a similar experience. As he sat in the hospital waiting room during his wife's caesarean section delivery, he was deeply concerned about how he would parent a daughter. Suddenly the swinging doors of the operating room banged open. There stood a nurse with a tiny, freshly born baby girl lying in a blanket, still messy from her arrival. This dad took one look at his new daughter and fell in love on the spot.

Love and Action

That father didn't have to worry about running out of love. But when it comes to expressing love, some dads seem to run out of gas.

Recently our staff received an interesting comment from a teenage girl about her relationship with her father. One of her statements really caught our attention: "All I know about my dad is that he is in a suit and he's successful."

This daughter perceives that her dad has it all together, but their relationship doesn't go much deeper than the surface. She probably doesn't know what drives him, what he's insecure about, what he values most, what his goals are, or what she means to him. Does he really love her?

Sadly, that kind of relationship is not unusual. It reminds me of another father, Joe, and his daughter. They attended one of our Father-Daughter Summits, where we try to help dads and their girls overcome barriers that keep them from connecting. Theirs was also a distant relationship—until they experienced that weekend together. Here's what Joe wrote about his experience:

> One major eye-opener for me happened during a lunch break. Earlier, during separate sessions, we were instructed to write our daughters a letter. I wrote about how she is beautiful, smart, talented, and a blessing to me. I filled a whole card! And I was amazed at how eager my daughter was to read it.
>
> Then, when we got back together again, she had a card she had written to me. I can't begin to describe what I felt as I read, *Dad, thank you for making me be here cuz I have learned a lot. And now I feel like I can talk to you about anything. I am looking forward to do something together again. Maybe next weekend. I just want to say I love you and thank you for being there for me.*

Joe's letter went on to say, "I cried. I simply cried. I'll never lose or let anything happen to the card I received from my daughter. It's very special to me because it came from someone very special in my life."

Learning to love our children means taking steps and making starts like that. If we open our hearts to our children, they'll often open theirs to us—especially if they're daughters.

Even when they're quite young, most girls are communicators. We need to give them opportunities. As soon as they can read and write, we can send them notes. We can let them know that we think about them frequently.

The notes don't have to be on paper, either. One of my favorite advertisements is for a cell phone that takes pictures. A dad is leaving on a trip; his little girl packs a toy monkey in his briefcase. He discovers his "traveling companion" on the way to the airport. He takes pictures of the monkey wherever he goes, sending them back home to his wife and daughter. Finally they get a picture on the computer showing the monkey in front of the house—and realize Daddy's home! That daughter knew her father was thinking constantly of her.

In one of our essay contests about fathers, one young woman wrote, "My dad holds the key to the unlocked door of my heart." That dad wasn't content to know that he loved his daughter. He let *her* know, too.

The Love-Your-Kids Chapter

When it comes to showing and telling our kids how much we love them, we dads often are so afraid of doing the wrong thing that we end up doing nothing. What are the right things to do? How do we put the love we feel and that we know we're supposed to give into action?

Well, there's a list. It's probably one you've heard before, though you may not have thought about how it relates to fathering. Many couples have the following Bible verses read at their wedding:

> Love is patient, love is kind. It does not envy, it does not boast, it is
> not proud. It is not rude, it is not self-seeking, it is not easily angered,
> it keeps no record of wrongs. Love does not delight in evil but rejoices
> with the truth. It always protects, always trusts, always hopes, always
> perseveres. (1 Corinthians 13:4-7)

I've found this list to be true and necessary when it comes to Championship Fathering. It's a great place to start when answering the question, "How do I love my kids?"

Love Is Patient

As I already mentioned, Melanie and I had three almost-grown kids when Chance arrived. This makes me a bit older than most fathers of 12-year-olds. I'm getting a do-over with Chance—and my older children sometimes kid me about how much I've changed as a dad.

I've tried to learn from mistakes I made earlier in my fathering efforts. I've also grown up some. And God has helped me to understand and appreciate my role as a father more than I did years ago. I love all my children, but I've noticed that the way I demonstrate love these days is sometimes different from the way I used to.

When young Chance disobeys or is just careless, I can deal with him more patiently than I did in my earlier years as a dad. I take more time to find out what he was thinking before I react.

Often I tell him, "Chance, the reason I seemed a little upset wasn't because you're so bad, or you did something so terrible. It's because I care for you. I'm concerned about what children go through today because of what some other people do to kids. My job as a father is to protect you until you become a man. That's why I need to talk with you when you make a mistake and even discipline you when you decide to disobey. And I can guarantee you're going to have these same talks and moments with your children someday."

A younger me might have reacted to Chance by laying down the law and passing out the punishment immediately. Those ingredients may still be in the recipe, but slowing down long enough to hear his side of the story keeps me from having to go back and apologize for overreacting or even jumping to the wrong conclusion.

This approach has also led to some great conversations. I get to understand my son better and he gets to understand me. He grasps the idea that when I discipline him I don't enjoy the painful part of it any more than he does—but I'm actually correcting him for his good, because I love him.

Love Is Kind

You've probably heard the phrase, "random acts of kindness." We dads need to be intentional about practicing those with our kids. Let's be unpredictable and *surprise* them with kindness!

So what is kindness? I think it's seeing and meeting someone's need—gently.

I've tried to do that in teaching Chance to learn responsibility. Since household chores are a great opportunity to do that, taking out the trash is a chore I've delegated to him.

I don't know about you, but I've found there's a lot more to chore delegation than just telling your child what to do. This is where kindness becomes a beautiful thing. I can say to Chance, "I'm asking you to do something important, and most of the time you may have to do it by yourself. But I want you to know that I enjoy working with you, so whenever possible, I'd like to take the trash out with you. And if there's more than you can handle some days, you can ask me to help you. Will you let me do that?"

This is a way to acknowledge your child's individuality. Some will insist on having help; others will want to do things by themselves. Either way is fine. Most kids, though, will appreciate the gentle approach that offers assistance.

Chores may be necessary housekeeping tasks, but we can express our appreciation to our kids for pitching in by kindly giving them unexpected perks. Chance and I both love a certain ice cream establishment in town; I make sure to give him unpredictable, random opportunities to join me for a cone, telling him how much I appreciate his efforts to do his part in our family life.

Not Envious, Boastful, Proud, or Rude

What do these have to do with loving your child? Quite a bit, actually.

Take envy. When your child was born, did you find yourself sometimes jealous of the special attention your wife gave to the baby—and didn't seem to have time to give to you? Even now, do you sometimes resent how much time kids require? Do those feelings seep out as impatience toward or distance from your child? Or do you gently admit the issue and talk about it with your bride?

Then there's boasting. When the family is talking about the day's successes, who goes first? Do you pay attention to your kids when they talk, or just itch for your chance to speak?

How about pride? I don't mean being pleased about our children and their achievements; that's part of loving them. The kind of pride that *isn't* loving is the one that convinces us we've got the parenting thing under control—and that we don't need to tell our kids we were wrong when we messed up. This pride rushes to find fault with others and overlooks faults in ourselves. Love steps up to admit failures.

As for rudeness—well, what do we do when our kids are long-winded, going on and on about things that may not seem too interesting to us? Do we interrupt them?

One evening not long ago, Chance called me from the other side of the house: "Dad, come down here!"

It sounded important, so I headed toward the sound of his voice. I found him standing by the back door. "Follow me, Dad," he said. "I have to show you something." Soon we were in the neighbor's yard, next to a large tree.

"What do you need, Son?" I asked.

"Watch this," he said. "Get your watch and time me."

He began climbing the tree. That had always been a challenge for Chance; now that he could do it, he just had to show me. He kept looking back down to see if I was watching.

That look of accomplishment on his little face stayed with me. If I'd been rude and ignored him because I was too busy or bored, I'd have missed it.

Nearly every day he's looking to me for validation and approval. He wants to know, *Are you watching me, Dad? Am I growing up to be a man? Am I making you proud?*

Similar moments happen all the time between dads and kids—in backyards, in gymnasiums, at spelling bees, and at dance recitals. When your kids check, are you watching? Since you love them, it would be rude not to give them that basic attention.

Not Self-Seeking

Chance came to me one day and said, "Daddy, Marcellus [his older brother] played football. You played football. I do not like football."

That was hard to hear. If there's one thing we dads think we know, it's how our kids should achieve. The first words that came to my mind were, "Come on, Son, you're going to strap on a helmet and pads and hit somebody!"

It had been easy for me to imagine Chance a little older and in football pads. His words made that dream pop like a soap bubble.

It got worse one evening when, as our staff at the National Center for Fathering sometimes does, I spoke to the players from the Kansas City Chiefs before a home game. I'd brought Chance along. Several of those 300-pound football players walked up to my son and asked, "Hey, Chance, you gonna play football one day?"

He answered without a moment's hesitation: "No, I don't like football."

I wanted in the worst way to yell, "Son, don't say that! That's Daddy's job you're putting at risk!" But the guys on the team took my son's rejection in stride.

A few days later, Chance came to me and looked me in the eye. His expression was very serious as he said, "Daddy, do you still like me and love me even though I don't play football?"

Before I could answer, he went on: "I see all your player stuff, Dad, in the Carolina room [a blue den at home where I spend a lot of time], and the pictures of you when you played football and all of that. But Daddy, do you like me? Do you love me?"

He really needed to know! He must have been thinking, *I came from you, Daddy. I look like you! I am your boy! But does your love depend on my playing football?*

Like Chance, your children need to know that you love them—in a way that doesn't demand its own way. They need your hugs. They need to hear, "I love you. If you can't chew bubble gum and walk straight, I still love you. If you don't have the same interests or skills I have, I still love you. You're my son. You're my daughter. No matter what, I love you."

Not Easily Angered; Keeps No Record of Wrongs

Some of us dads have short tempers and long memories.

At times we get frustrated out there in the world, where we may constantly be interrupted and disrespected. Perhaps we come home from work each day with a huge chip on our shoulder and tell ourselves that interruptions and disrespect are things we shouldn't have to put up with there.

Attitudes like irritability—which we wouldn't dare project at work—we often feel free to spread around generously to family members, especially our kids. But if we can control those attitudes at work, we can control them at home. Those we love shouldn't have to pay double for the bruises we get along the way.

We can replace irritable words with encouraging ones. When I played ball in high school, I used to run back punts and kickoffs. I vividly remember a few times when our team was behind or in a close game, and our coach instilled great confidence in me through his words. Waiting for the kickoff, I'd hear him say, "We need one, Carey. Run it back for us." He was depending on me, and his urging helped me focus and dig a little deeper, reaching for excellence.

There's great power in words, especially from fathers. As Proverbs 12:18 puts it, "Reckless words pierce like a sword, but the tongue of the wise brings healing." Your words have that kind of power with your children. They'll remember many of your statements for years to come. Much of their outlook on life could be determined by what you say—for better or for worse.

You can challenge and inspire as my coach did. Or you can be reckless with your words.

Ever heard yourself saying something like, "What are you *thinking*?" or, "Can't you do *anything* right?"

Sometimes the tone of voice is more damaging than the words themselves. Some dads intentionally use an irritated tone, wanting to make it clear how bothersome their kids are being—or thinking that sounding vexed will motivate children to improve. But remember that you can catch more flies with honey than with vinegar. Kids respond much better to positive words than to criticism, preaching, or nagging.

Does Not Delight in Evil; Rejoices with the Truth

We'll look more closely at this when we discuss coaching and modeling. For now, I'll just say that love cheers for the truth and for what's right. It doesn't try to excuse doing the wrong thing, even wrongs that promise to make us feel better.

Take profanity, for instance. When the hammer hits the thumb or the driver on his cell phone swerves in front of us, the temptation to let off steam in a cloud of "colorful" words may be overwhelming. But our kids listen carefully to how we talk. They're like sponges when it comes to picking up expressions we use, particularly those that shock us when we hear them coming out of our children's mouths.

Loving our children means, among other things, deciding we won't use language that we don't want them to use. And since they watch carefully whose side we're on, it also means choosing heroes we'd be glad to have them imitate.

Protects, Trusts, Hopes, Perseveres

The 2006 movie *The Pursuit of Happyness,* starring Will Smith, portrays a father's commitment to his son in the middle of very difficult circumstances. Looking at the life of this dad, Chris Gardner, some people might find some things they don't approve of. But there's also much to admire in the experiences of a homeless man fighting to make life better for himself and his young son.

Chris Gardner went on to reap the benefits of his hard work and determination, becoming a success in the world of stock trading and benevolence. His son would eventually say, "I never knew we were poor, because everywhere I turned, I saw my dad."

Isn't that interesting? Statistics show that if a dad isn't there, his children are more likely to be poor. This child *was* very poor, but didn't know it *because his dad was there.*

The one constant in that boy's life was his father's presence. That dad did everything in his power to protect his son from harm, provide hope, and persevere to give the boy a better opportunity. That's the kind of security we provide as loving fathers.

I think about this a lot regarding Chance. The other night I was putting him to bed and lay down next to him. We turned on some Christian music that had a good beat, and we were just listening and talking. After awhile I asked, "Chance, why do you like doing this?"

And he said, "I just like being with you, Dad."

At times like that it's clear that my son feels secure with me. I was fortunate to have that feeling with my dad, no matter what we were doing—just being with him made me feel safe.

Your children gain confidence from your consistent, loving presence. Instead of leaving them doubting, waiting, and wondering, be there. Make sure they understand that nothing they can do will make you stop loving them.

Love That Listens

There's one more action I'd like to add to this "love list."

Not long ago, I helped out with one of our Father-Daughter Summit events. We asked daughters to complete anonymously this statement directed to their dads: "I wish you would _____."

We received a variety of responses, but were overwhelmed by the common theme that emerged: *listening.*

Communication is a common challenge for dads and teenage daughters, and there are always two sides to it. But we fathers need to get the ball rolling.

Here are some things those girls said about listening:

- "I wish my dad would try to understand what I'm going through, and be there when I need someone to talk to just as a friend and not as a parent."
- "I need him to completely hear me out and not assume things . . . to listen before he speaks."
- "[I wish he] would take time and not talk but let me tell him one secret that I have hidden for a long time."
- "Try to see where I'm coming from before blowing up in my face and later wanting my forgiveness."
- "Listen when I need you to. You don't have to have the right answers all the time; just be there for me."
- "I wish my dad would just listen to me and not try to make everything about him."
- "If my dad would listen and forgive me without always a punishment, I would open up and tell him more! I don't because I'm scared of getting grounded."
- "Actually stop and listen . . . don't think about what you're going to say, but hear and understand what I'm saying."
- "Listen to me [without trying] to fix the problem or discipline me for it, but just listen."

One girl wrote simply, "Don't talk; don't argue; just listen."

I think you get the point. Listening is one of the greatest steps toward bonding with your child.

And it's not only for daughters, either. Not long ago, my son Chance and I were having a confrontation (yes, those happen in my house, too). He'd disobeyed, and I'd gotten into domineering mode—determined to get my way and put him in his place.

But in the midst of those heated emotions, I sensed I was missing something. Maybe God was working on me. I slowed down, calmed down, and tried something new—listening.

"Chance," I said, "let's talk about this. Tell me what you're going through. What are you thinking and feeling right now?"

His response surprised me: "Dad, you don't really want to hear what I say. You really don't care, and you don't want to know."

Do I need to learn something here? I thought.

"Son, tell me more," I replied. "I'm ready to listen right now."

We talked a little more. Gradually it came out that he didn't feel free to express himself without being judged or even a little intimidated.

It got me thinking. As fathers, we sometimes abuse our position of authority. It's easy to do unintentionally. We can fall into a pattern of insisting on the first and last words. If we take this approach, though, pretty soon no one will be listening to us!

As with Chance, I believe every child wants a dad who's approachable and listens. Part of unconditional love is being genuinely interested in how our kids feel and what they're going through.

From time to time, especially when our children are young, we need to step back and think about how they see us—giants who tower over them and have such power! It helps to literally get down to their level and speak face-to-face—and listen.

Championship Checklist

Ultimately, the question isn't so much whether I love my children. It's this: Do they *know* I love them?

At the National Center for Fathering our research has identified seven statements that can help us track whether we're communicating love to our children. Taken together, they're a checklist you can consult from time to time to see how you're doing.

1. *I praise my children for the things they do well.* Face it: Some of us dads demand a standard of excellence from our kids that we could never meet ourselves. It's easy to develop a habit of "constructive criticism" that makes our kids feel they can't do anything right.

Here's a little experiment: Make a list of the top five things each of your children does really well. This may be a little harder than you think. Once you have the lists, make it a point to mention those things when you notice an example in your child's life—and on other occasions, too.

Do you wonder if this really would make an impact on your child's life? Imagine how it would feel to have *your* father pull you aside and say something like, "I was thinking about how much I love you, and I made this list of things that I think you really do well."

Kids can't get too old to be touched by a message like that. Though I'm now a grandfather, I can't begin to describe how much it would mean to have a conversation like that with my dad right now.

2. *I express affection to my children.* There are many ways to do this, but I'm amazed how often grown children tell me they've never had a parent say to them, "I love you." That's a start. If you don't say those words, then how *do* your kids know you love them?

Maybe your upbringing makes it almost impossible for you to say the words without choking up or going numb. Well, work on it! This isn't about you; it's about what your kids need, right?

Start with notes ("Dad loves you") left in unusual places (a bathroom mirror, inside a laptop, on a pillow). Describe both discipline and good times as examples of love ("Do you know why I'm doing this? Because I love you").

Patient repetition is important. Find all the ways you can to make the point that you love your child; don't trust osmosis.

3. *I tell my children they are special to me.* This is particularly important when you have more than one child. Each needs to know your love for him or her isn't generic but individual. You love that uniqueness, those special characteristics that can't be replaced or compared. If you made a "Top Five Things Each of My Children Does Well" list for #1, that could come in handy here.

Make each child your "favorite" in his or her own way. The conversation might go like this:

"You're my favorite daughter with brown eyes!"

"Dad! I'm your only daughter with brown eyes!"

"Exactly! You're my favorite in that category!"

4. *I have a close bond with my child.* Some of this can happen without

trying—for example, if you and your child share a distinct characteristic like being left-handed. But most of it comes from decisions on your part, experiences you share, moments that forever bind you.

For one father, such a moment came while he was introducing one of his boys to primitive camping—sleeping under the stars on an open tarp. During the night a rainstorm opened up on the two of them. The father threw half the tarp over his son and himself as an instant cover and went back to sleep—only to realize later that night that his son had slipped out from under the tarp and was soaking wet. He pulled the boy into his sleeping bag, lying on his back with his son on his chest. The boy shivered, but gradually fell back to sleep. That unplanned moment bound them as father and son.

We need to find times and places where bonding can take place. They're easier to find when we regularly participate in the things our kids like to do.

5. *I tell my children I am proud of them.* As I've already mentioned, Jesus benefited when His Father said, "This is my Son, whom I love; with him I am well pleased" (Matthew 3:17). If you never heard your father tell someone else, "I'm proud of my son," I'm sure you feel you've missed something.

I guarantee your kids will not get tired of hearing you say to them—and to others—that you're proud of them. Find ways to make it specific: qualities, traits, abilities, actions of which you're proud. Note when they do something pleasantly surprising and let them know how that made you feel: "When I saw you stop and help that kid who'd tripped instead of laughing at him like the others were doing, I wanted to tell everybody you were my son."

6. *I carefully listen to my children express their concerns.* The important word here is *carefully.*

I find it far too easy to listen carelessly to Chance. I can't multitask when he's talking to me; I need to pay attention. Otherwise, I'll miss the message behind the words—and I won't ask the kind of questions I should when he's done talking.

Here's a little test of your listening skills. As soon as your son or daughter is finished telling you something, say, "This is what I just heard you say." Then repeat in your own words what he or she said.

This sounds easy, but it isn't. This exercise in active listening can help your child speak more effectively, and especially help you listen better!

7. *I point out qualities in my children that I like about them.* Here's another good use for that list from #1. In addition to noting attitudes and actions that make you feel good, you can also point out those you want to work on because your kids are ahead of you!

Here's an example: "When I saw how you shared your gift with your brother, it made me think that I need to do a better job of sharing what I have with others. I really like that quality in you."

I hope you'll try using this checklist, and the others that appear elsewhere in this book. Even those of us involved in research on fathering find these statements a real source of accountability when it comes to our own lives as dads.

Not So Mysterious

Love, as the song once said, is a many-splendored thing. But it's no mystery, especially where our kids are concerned.

Research and experience tell us that practical love for our kids is a doable proposition for fathers. It's also a tough-edged pursuit that involves a lot of thinking, taking time, talking, and touching.

Opportunities to apply love in your home will keep coming up, every day and when you least expect them. That means you'll get plenty of practice—a good thing, since a dad involved in Championship Fathering wants to be a continuously improving practitioner of love for his children.

 ACTION POINTS

How to Love Your Child

Preschool
- Have a playful staring contest with your child, making every effort to communicate love with your eyes.

- Take part in some of the daily routines of caring for your child (bathtime, bedtime, tooth-brushing, etc.). Include lots of verbal affirmations.
- Call your child while you're at work just to say "Hi" and "I miss you."
- Notice and praise a job well done, or progress your child has made. Tell him or her, "I'm proud to be your dad."
- If you have an infant, provide lots of positive eye contact. It's a major source of emotional security for him or her.
- Plan some time every day to simply play with your child—even if it's just for a few minutes.
- Get down on your child's level to give your undivided attention whenever you're listening.
- Be physically active with your kids, which often builds relationships by leading to playful interaction.
- Make sure your little one is very familiar with you—your face, your touch, your voice.

Elementary
- Tell your child (or write in a letter), "I'm glad you're my son/daughter. You're very important to me, and I'm going to do all I can to help you become the person God has created you to be."
- Honor your child by throwing a "just because" party with the theme, "I love you for no particular reason—just because."
- Write a note to your child that points out a specific strength in a sport or hobby he or she enjoys.
- Pay careful attention to how you talk to your children—not only the words, but also tone and volume. Make every effort to be positive; avoid being even mildly sarcastic or degrading.
- If you can't be with your kids as often as you'd like, record and send each of them an audio or video message. Or write notes listing 10 things you love about them.

- Write affirming notes and hide them for your children to find later—perhaps much later.
- Affirm a specific character trait in your child. Then add a comment like, "But I love you no matter what."

Teen
- Give your child a 10-second hug.
- Write your child a letter listing at least three things you appreciate about him or her, or with a blessing specific to his or her character.
- Give your child plenty of nonverbal affirmations: pats on the back, a shoulder massage, a squeeze of the arm, etc.
- Use milestone events—graduations, performances, sports events, getting a summer job—to communicate to your child verbally, "I love you just as you are, and I'm proud to be your dad."
- Take advantage of opportunities to praise your child in front of others.
- Give each member of your family five sincere compliments this week. Do it by leaving notes, sending e-mails or text messages, or in other creative ways.
- Learn to do something your child loves: a video game, a sport, playing the guitar, making a music video, etc.
- Leave your child a note of encouragement. Slip it into his or her backpack, send a text message, or post it on his or her social networking Internet site.

For additional practical tips on fathering, subscribe to the National Center for Fathering's free e-mail, *fathers.com weekly,* at www.fathers.com/weekly. You'll also find articles on a wide range of fathering situations and challenges at www.fathers.com.

CHAPTER SIX

Loving Your Children's Mother

L oving our kids starts long before they're born. If we want to truly love them, we start by loving their mother.

It's obvious that a lot of people are missing this. But a protected-by-marriage love ought to be in place when children are conceived, and that same shelter of love remains the ideal environment in which to raise kids to maturity.

Even though folks are trying to do this parenting thing in every other way possible, it's not hard to see that the system was designed for a man and woman to make a child and then raise that child. If we men can't even become fathers without a woman's help, it makes sense to recognize that Championship Fathering will also involve a woman.

A Note to Divorced and Never-Married Dads

If you're reading this as a dad who's divorced or never married, you may wonder how this applies to you. It's not my purpose here to assign blame or to offer a fix for your situation. But I can say that you, too, need to account for your children's mother in your efforts to be an effective father. I will keep your situation in mind as we look at the challenges of a father loving his children by loving his wife, so stay with me.

I believe that even when a marriage has been destroyed by the tragedy of divorce, a father must treat the mother of his children with a respect that shelters those children. This is also true of dads who have fathered children but have not married the mother.

I know the past can't be changed or erased. If you're a divorced or never-married father, some of what I have to say in this chapter may frustrate you. I can't help that. But I can encourage you to keep your eye on the goal—your kids. They deserve a dad who doesn't throw in the towel on fatherhood. You and your children's mother may stand on opposite sides of a huge emotional gulf, but I know you don't want to see your kids fall into it.

For the sake of your children, practice respect for their mother. Wherever possible, develop a spirit of cooperation. Resist the tendency to take a hard line toward each other; it may seem that the relationship is dead and over, but the children who are living proof of that relationship still desperately need your recognition, care, and parenting.

Avoid condemning your children's mother, particularly in their presence. Work at making your conversations with her about the children a no-jab and no-blame zone, where you set aside personal issues for the mutual goal of seeing your children healthy and whole.

A Championship Challenge

"Husbands, love your wives." Simple, right? We asked them to marry us because we loved them. We vowed in the wedding ceremony that we would love them, and it's hard to come up with a believable explanation that lets us off the hook for our promises. If I'm a husband, one of my number-one jobs is to love my wife.

So how do we approach this challenge? By figuring out what kind of chocolate she likes? By remembering her favorite flowers? By getting an administrative assistant or computer to remind us when the anniversary is coming up?

For many of us, loving our wives seems like a problem to be solved, a mystery to be unraveled. This is where we sometimes get off track; loving our wives is not a puzzle, it's a pattern to discover and maintain for a lifetime.

Our research often points to the overwhelming need for a father to love and respect the mother of his children. How do you start? If you're married and haven't done this lately, listen up. Tonight, I want you to go home, and—whether your lips are as big as mine or not—walk in and plant a big one on your bride right in front of your kids.

They'll probably react. Expect to hear, "Oooh, Dad! What are you doing? I can't look!"

Don't let them intimidate you! They may be a little embarrassed, but they need to see passion and deep love in your marriage. They might not ask, but they do wonder if you love their mom. The evidence of an unbreakable and healthy bond between you and your wife is a wall of security around them.

I'll never forget when we discovered our youngest son, Chance, was on the way. My son Marcellus was about 13 years old, coming home from summer camp. I went to meet the bus at the church.

Driving home, I said, "Marcellus, did you have a good time at camp?"

"Yeah, Dad, I had a great time. How was your week?"

"I had a great week. And by the way, Son, I gotta tell you some news. Mommy and Daddy are with child."

"What? What do you mean?"

"Mom's pregnant."

He let that settle in for a moment. Then he said, "Ugh! No way, Dad! Shoot me straight. That's not true, is it?"

Chuckling, I explained, "Yeah, Mom's pregnant, man. Dad ain't just been preaching the last three months."

Marcellus leaned against the window and shook his head. "Oooh, gross, Dad. You mean y'all still do that?" At the time we had three kids, so he must have thought we'd "had fun" just three times.

"Homey," I said, "let me school you up. God made sex. Hugh Hefner didn't make sex. Larry Flynt, Son, didn't make sex. That lying stuff on the computer, that billion-dollar industry called pornography, is a lie. That's counterfeit. Buddy, God made sex! It's not bad! It's one of the greatest joys God made to bring husband and wife together. It's in His plan for pleasure as well as procreation. I'm shooting you straight, Son. You're gonna have a brother or sister."

Somehow both of us survived that conversation.

It's up to us to communicate to our children what marriage and romantic love are all about. We do it best by example—showing love to our brides and serving them. We also teach our kids by talking about it when opportunities come up. Let's make sure they get a clear picture of marriage from God's perspective.

I Love You

We can train ourselves to say "I love you" to our wives, but we don't want to say those words just because they're a requirement. We can come up with loving reasons for making statements whether or not they're tied to feelings. So think about saying, "I love you"—but don't say, "I think I love you"!

Try turning to your wife and saying, "I've got something very important I have to tell you—I love you." The fact that you've placed some emphasis on this may provoke an unusual response.

Be prepared to answer the "Why?" question when you tell your wife you love her. Answer the question sometimes without being asked. Before she can say anything, add, "Do you want to know why I love you?"

You'll have her undivided attention. She won't be able to wait to hear what you'll say next, so make it good! Give the next three sentences you say some careful thought. Make them your own. Here are a few questions to help you through that process.

Why are you content in a love relationship with this woman? Because she challenges you to be a better man? Because she's an amazing mother to your children? Because of the way she understands and repeatedly forgives you? Because of what she's taught you about love? Be prepared to give at least three brief statements to back up your declaration of love.

When you communicate love to your wife, focus on how she thinks and feels about love rather than your own confusion and difficulty. Maybe words don't really "say" love to her. To find that out, become an attentive student of your woman. It doesn't hurt to ask, "What words or actions communicate love to you most clearly, Babe?" Or even, "Would you tell me about some times in your life when you really felt loved?" You may be surprised at how specific she is.

Sometimes we miss the mark in expressing love, and it hurts to find that out. We can bring chocolates home every week, only to discover that she feels fat rather than loved. We might buy flowers, then hear that she'd rather we volunteered to do the dishes. The road to learning is paved with little failures like these, but we have to get over them.

Once we find out what makes our woman feel loved and secure, we've got to get busy making sure she gets plenty of it! She's probably not going to give you a list, though. Even if she does, do your best not to let her know you're working from it.

If she says, "When you take care of something that's broken around the house or carry out the garbage without my asking, that makes me feel loved," don't make your response obvious. When she isn't looking, do the things she mentions. Don't wear a "Mr. Fix-it" T-shirt and put a neon sign on your forehead that flashes, "Watch me take out this trash, Baby!"

Your children will be watching most of this. They'll be "catching" it in ways they may not even be aware of. They won't think, *I'll have to remember this for later.* But someday they'll do something for their spouse and it will dawn on them: *This is just what Dad used to do for Mom.*

Watching the way you treat their mother will create an invisible but indelible record in their hearts and minds.

Tough Love

Love between a husband and wife is more than cuddling by a fireplace, talking about what makes you feel good. Sometimes it's the *opposite* of staying warm and toasty. There's a toughness that complements the tenderness.

My dad had that kind of commitment to my mother. I remember how that played out one frosty Sunday morning in Virginia.

The family car had broken down, but my mother needed groceries. Breakfast was in jeopardy. Pop said, "Come on, boys. You're coming with me." I can still hear his wing-tip shoes crunching on the gravel as he walked toward the store and we followed him.

It wasn't what I wanted to do that morning, but the experience stuck with me. It still comes to mind when I think of a husband showing love to his bride. It's not the classic picture of love between man and wife, and probably wouldn't make much of a scene in a romance novel or TV movie. But it was real. Even as a thickheaded adolescent I could sense love in what Pop was doing.

Sometimes love means doing things you don't feel like doing. Besides hiking for groceries on a cold morning, it's washing the dishes or laundry, getting up at 3 A.M. to feed the new baby (or getting the baby so your wife can nurse, then offering to put the little one back to bed).

Sometimes love feels like drudgery. It's a daily grind! It's more about perseverance than it is about songs and sighs. As numerous authors have correctly pointed out, it's a choice we keep making and a decision that comes up continuously. It isn't something we do because it makes us feel good or because we think we're going to be rewarded. It focuses entirely on the other person.

Now, don't get me wrong. Romance is a good thing. It was designed by God to bring husbands and wives closer. Flowers, date nights, pet names, and sex are a big part of marriage. But they're not everything.

If your bride is truly a high priority, the way you value her should be seen in the way you serve her—the hard work, the sacrifices, the inconveniences. Think of her first, tune in to her needs, and follow through.

Long-Term Love

What happens between two people who spend a lifetime loving each other? It's not hard for me to picture. I have many good memories of just such a marriage, thanks to the example of my mom and dad.

When my brother and I were little, we'd go into our parents' room on Saturday mornings. Mom and Dad would be hugged up under the covers, sleeping. So we'd climb on the chest of drawers and jump onto their bed.

Boom! Boom! Their mattress took a lot of abuse. For us, that was the official beginning of weekend fun.

Somehow our frolicking didn't bother them. They seemed oblivious to us, and I could tell those early morning moments were a time of real intimacy for them.

Fast-forward about 40 years. My parents had grown old. My mother had just undergone emergency heart bypass surgery. My dad had been living nearby at a care center for several years; his Parkinson's disease had made it impossible for him to stay at home.

I flew to Virginia to see Mom, who had made it through the operation just fine. I needed to see Dad, too.

I hadn't told Dad I was coming. We knew that in his condition, he couldn't spend long hours with us in the hospital waiting room, and we didn't want to worry him—so we hadn't told him about the operation. When I walked into his room, he said, "Hey, Son. What's wrong?" He knew an unannounced arrival meant unexpected news.

"Mom's been sick," I said, "but she's fine now, Dad. She just had bypass surgery."

He looked into the distance for a moment. Finally he said, "Help dress me, Son. Take me to her." Though he was declining in his capacities, he still wanted to be there for his bride.

I drove him to the hospital and wheeled him down the hall to Mom's room.

The doctors said Mom was doing well, though she didn't look that way.

Lying in bed, she was very alert but couldn't talk because of all the tubes and breathing devices.

But when she saw her man come through the door, it was as though I wasn't in the room. She spoke with her eyes.

Daddy made soft, comforting noises, feeling her pain.

Despite the fact that Mom had wires everywhere and an IV in her arm, she reached her hand through the bed railing. Dad held it tenderly. Shaking from the Parkinson's, he managed to hang on. Their hands moved in rhythm.

I stood there watching them with tears rolling down my cheeks. I remembered vividly those moments as a boy when I jumped off the dresser onto their bed and they were in a world of their own.

They were still intimate after all these years. If you'll pardon the expression, they were still *making love*.

Thinking of those moments now makes me realize how much they gave me as a child because of their love. I'm determined to honor their example in the way I love my bride with faithfulness and intimacy throughout my life.

The Imperfect Present

Even though I have powerful memories of my parents to motivate me, however, I don't have the love-your-wife thing mastered. That was obvious recently when I came home after a long day of work, eager to get in a comfortable chair and read the newspaper.

Soon my bride, Melanie, walked in and said, "Sweetheart, would you go and get some gas in my car?"

My first thought was, *Gas for her car? I've had a long day. And it's summer; she has time to do those things!*

I suspect the look on my face gave away what I was thinking. But my wife knows me, so she let me mull things over for a while.

At times like this, when it's basically all about Carey, it's almost like I get a personal visit from God about my attitude. This time the "conversation" went something like this: "Okay, Carey. So, you're the CEO of the National

Center for Fathering? Big deal! You've had a busy day? Let me tell you, Boy, Melanie's schedule would eat you up! You're Ralph and Sarah's son? What would they think right now?"

I've found that I can argue with God—but I can't win. Especially when I hear the clincher: "Okay, Carey, you say you want to be an example to your children and the neighbors? Here's your chance."

Being the bright person I am, I got the message. And I got the gas.

I know Melanie would never go public or sit around with her friends and say, "My husband said this, but he doesn't live it." But she's praying to God and knows He'll keep me in line. Her attitude is, "I ain't worried about you, Boy, because you have to answer to the heavenly Father if you don't take care of the basics." That holds my attention.

Incidents like that get me thinking, *God forbid that I would not be grateful for the privilege of serving my bride by going to get gas in her car.* I have close friends who've lost their wives to cancer or other tragedies. What do you think they'd give for the chance to do their brides a small favor like that?

You and I should be eager to serve the women God has given us—in big and small ways. Make the bed when you can. Fold the socks and underwear, and help with other chores. Ask if you can bring her something from the kitchen.

Love's not about what's convenient or easy. It finds a way to serve.

Listen to Your Love

Just as we need to listen as fathers, we need to listen as husbands.

Why? First, our wives tell us valuable information about themselves. Second, they inform us about the kids with motherly intuition we dare not ignore. Third, they have crucial words to say about *us.*

Recently Melanie and I went out for an evening walk—and a talk. Like the amazing, godly woman she is, she lovingly confronted me about a few things.

She gently told me I wasn't leaving work thoughts and responsibilities at the office. Not that I was letting my job dominate my home life, but I was more preoccupied with work than I should have been. "I'm just telling you what you've been preaching to fathers and to your staff," she said.

That stung a bit. But we continued talking about goals and our children. Her final words on that subject were profound: "Baby, you're going to have to catch a ball with Chance. Nobody else can do that like you can."

I'd played ball with my older son, Marcellus, but Melanie had noticed that I hadn't been doing the same with Chance. Already Chance had told me he didn't think he was cut out for football, and I didn't want to pressure him to follow in my footsteps. But my bride pointed out that Chance would still enjoy throwing the ball around with me. She was schooling me up, helping me see what I was too close to see.

There are two lessons here. First, our kids need us. Second, we need our wives to hold us accountable. They can keep us in check and let us know when we need to make adjustments in our fathering.

Working side-by-side with my bride makes me a better father as I love her and respect her. I'm thankful for her unique insights, and that we make a great team. Listening to Melanie has reminded me that Championship Fathering is only part of Championship Parenting!

Championship Checklist

Here's another list of statements based on research by the National Center for Fathering. They can help you evaluate how you're doing at loving your children's mother—a crucial part of Championship Fathering. Not all of these apply to divorced dads, but everyone can at least consider the first four.

1. *I discuss my children's development with my children's mother.* These conversations keep moms and dads on the same page, since effective parenting has a lot to do with coordinated efforts. Our children feel deeply loved when they realize their parents are united in raising them.

Discussions about discipline and other subjects over which you may disagree shouldn't be conducted within hearing range of the kids. We need to work through parenting differences in private; subjecting our kids to them makes children feel unsettled.

Here's one strange phenomenon—expressing a real interest in our children's development is something many wives find very romantic. It makes sense when you think about it; we're discussing the living products of earlier romance!

2. *I discuss my goals for each child with my children's mother.* This assumes you *have* specific goals and dreams for each of your children. If you don't, ask yourselves this: By the time they're 18, what kind of young adults do you want them to be?

If one goal is that your kids will be wise money managers, you and your children's mother can talk about the role of allowance, work, spending, and other issues. Teaching your children about money may force you to learn a lot more about it yourself!

3. *I discuss my children's problems with my children's mother.* The challenge is to agree with your spouse that the point of talking about your children's problems isn't to decide whose fault they are!

Often we don't get anywhere near helping our kids because we're so intent on blaming each other. Assigning blame quickly or refusing to accept it doesn't make things better.

Focus on seeing the problem and brainstorming solutions. Take shared responsibility for responding. And remember that the older the child is, the more responsibility he or she needs to accept for dealing with the problem.

Our children's struggles can drive us apart or drive us together. They make us feel inadequate; after all, we're humans, not superheroes. Wise parents realize they need help.

One of the greatest resources available to a couple is prayer. Talking to God about your concerns for your children can put you both on the same page in creating a plan of action.

4. *I discuss my frustrations as a parent with my children's mother.* Our aggravations sometimes reveal that we had unrealistic expectations about how we'd perform as parents. Children have an amazing capacity for revealing

our insecurities. A healthy discussion about parental irritations should include a healthy dose of encouragement for our partner.

If you're feeling disappointed as a father, it's likely your wife shares many similar frustrations—and then some. Appreciate who she is as a mother; point out things you think she's doing well. She's probably a lot harder on herself than you could be, so keep the "constructive criticism" to a minimum.

Prayer is important in this area, too. If you're regularly talking with God about your frustrations as a parent, let your children's mother listen in and even join the conversation.

5. *I spend time with my wife away from the children.* Take the lead on this. Make arrangements for sitters and "escape locations." Believe it or not, calling a sitter can be a romantic thing to do for your wife.

The child-rearing years may seem to go on forever. But eventually the two of you will again be seated as a couple at the breakfast table. There will be no kids to feed, dress, or get out the door for school—just you and your spouse.

When that day comes, you don't want to feel like you're sitting across from a stranger. Plan and spend couple time on a regular basis.

6. *I have a good relationship with my wife.* "Good" isn't what you want to aim for or settle for. That should be the default setting in your marriage.

You also don't want the "graph" of your marriage to have radical ups and downs, going from terrible to miserable to great to ho-hum. Aim for the "floor" to be good. On your "bad" days, your relationship still should be good. On top of good you can build better and great!

A good marriage doesn't mean you never argue. It means you've decided you won't end your days angry, but will settle your disagreements before you go to sleep. A good marriage isn't one that avoids all difficulties; it's one in which you learn to handle them, knowing that many of them can't be avoided!

7. *I am romantic with my wife.* The issue isn't whether I think I'm being romantic with my wife; it's whether she thinks I'm being romantic with her.

For many of us men, romance is a long detour to our destination when we were hoping for a shortcut. Here's a clue, though. The conversation you have with your wife about what she thinks is romantic may be one of the most romantic things you've ever done for her!

Consider asking her, "Honey, what are some of the things you've heard husbands have done for their wives that you really thought were romantic?" Don't keep notes while she's talking, but do whatever you need to later so that you don't forget what she told you. She's just given you a glimpse of how she spells R-O-M-A-N-C-E.

8. *I have a sexually fulfilling relationship with my wife.* If you can't make this statement, have you talked to your wife about your needs and expectations?

We men usually admit we're clueless when it comes to the role and details of romance. Women often feel the same way about sex. It's not that they can't enjoy it as much as we do; it's that they think of it differently. For us, it's always somewhere in the picture; for them it may be completely absent.

Remember that *talking* about this and *complaining* about this are two very different ways to communicate. The first one has a much better chance of creating delightful results.

Keep the Love Boat Afloat

Each of the items on that checklist can have a huge impact on your progress in Championship Fathering. Your children's mother desperately needs to see and hear you loving her children—and your children will experience your love in the deepest ways as they observe you loving their mother.

Marriage maintenance and improvement is a leadership responsibility for all married dads. At the next opportunity—Valentine's Day, for instance— I challenge you to honor your bride in a big way, even as you work to honor her every day. Pull out all the stops. Make her feel special. Buy gifts, make dinner reservations, even schedule a weekend away if your budget allows. Your creativity can make Valentine's Day—or any other day—special.

Make it a point to thank and praise your bride *in front of your children*. Tell her how she makes you a better man and father. Be specific. Think of five things you've learned from her over the years and thank her for her partnership, caring, and insight.

Love your wife—first, out of obedience because God commands us to love our wives as Christ loved the church and gave Himself for her. Then do it because it strengthens your marriage—which was also part of God's design.

All the while you'll be setting an example, creating memories and expectations that your children will take into their own marriages.

 ACTION POINTS

How to Love Your Children's Mother

- Do something special for your wife this week: Get her long-stemmed roses, arrange a surprise date night, write a love letter, etc.
- Devise a secret sign that you and your spouse can use to help each other recognize when emotions are escalating during a conflict.
- Ask how you can relieve some of the pressure your children's mom feels as a mother.
- Honor your children's mom in their presence. Compliment her often and make sure your children show her respect.
- Have a "state of the union" discussion with your wife. Ask her what you can do to help build a better marriage.
- Schedule a time when you and your wife can get away alone and do something fun together.
- Compliment your wife for using one of her spiritual gifts or for a way in which she is serving others.
- Are you a divorced dad? It's still important for you to show respect to your kids' mom and encourage them to honor her. Help them plan for Mother's Day—in May or at any other time of year.
- Thank your wife for a specific way in which she helps you to be a better dad.

- Plan an outing or vacation with your wife, aiming to make it an experience she'll remember fondly for a long, long time.
- Enlist your kids' help in doing something special for their mother, whether it's making a gift, shopping for one, or cleaning the house.
- Ask your children what qualities they're looking for in a future mate. Often their answers will reflect something about your marriage.

For additional practical tips on fathering, subscribe to the National Center for Fathering's free e-mail, *fathers.com weekly,* at www.fathers.com/weekly. You'll also find articles on a wide range of fathering situations and challenges at www.fathers.com.

CHAPTER SEVEN

Coaching

Playing football in high school and college happened decades ago for me. So it's kind of funny that my "claim to fame," you might say, took place in the year 2000. That was when the movie *Remember the Titans* came out in theaters.

I didn't appear in the movie. But you could say I lived it out to a degree. In real life, I was on the team that played the Titans in that 1971 Virginia state championship game that's the climax of the film.

My team was actually from a different high school than the one that appears in the movie. The script names Marshall, another team in the conference that played the Titans a good game earlier in the year. But in the historic championship game, I have to admit the Titans beat us—27 to nothing.

So, if you watch the movie and see a little white guy running back kicks against the Titans, that was me . . . sort of. But I did know Gerry Bertier and Julius Campbell, those two standout defensive players for the Titans. And I got to play on an all-star team for Coach Boone, the character played by Denzel Washington.

Coach Boone and I still talk from time to time. His approach to coaching reminds me a lot of what I want to do as a father—which is the subject of this chapter.

Everybody's a Coach

Everywhere I go, whenever I start talking sports with men, I soon realize I'm surrounded by coaches.

For most of us, rooting for a team involves imagining ourselves as a coach of that team. We have very definite ideas about what we would have done in certain situations or memorable games. Many of us seem to think that if we'd been on the sidelines, we'd have made better decisions than the coach who was actually there!

Having had the privilege of getting to know a few NFL coaches, I've learned that part of the "territory" is dealing with constant second-guessing by fans. I've heard more than one coach say, "You know, if *I* had several hours to think about it, heard multiple opinions from sportscasters, and could watch countless instant replays of the play I called—I probably wouldn't have called that play, either!"

Hindsight coaching doesn't make many mistakes. Real-time coaching deals with the pressures of life and the limitations of not being able to see the future.

Fathering involves real-time coaching. Championship Fathering requires a *lot* of it.

We may never walk the sidelines of a professional football field or pace the hardwood floor in Madison Square Garden during an NBA game. But our coaching challenge as dads is infinitely more important. Teams come and go, and sports are just sports, but our children are for keeps. They're immortal beings whose destinies we help to shape.

Coaching is about participating, not being a spectator. It recognizes that you've traveled further down the road of life than your child has. It acknowledges that you can greatly improve your kids' experiences if you give them the benefit of yours.

Many of us think we'd do a better job of growing up if we could go back and start over. That's never going to happen. But Championship Fathering allows us to help the children we love to avoid some mistakes that make us wish we could do life over again!

Coach Dad

I've had the opportunity to play under various coaches. Each had a personality and style all his own and left an impression on my life. But I can now see that all but one were like assistant coaches, working under my Pop's supervision.

My dad was always the head coach, often backing up and validating what other coaches tried to teach me. Many times it was Pop who helped me see that the principles that worked on the playing field also worked in life. He was the coach behind my coaches.

I've already mentioned that in high school I was about to quit a team because my friends and I thought the coach was unfair; we interpreted his decisions as racist. But my dad stepped in and made sure I understood that if I was as good as I thought, the coach would have every reason to let me play. The coach's decisions were based on sound philosophy and a pretty good understanding of my abilities—not a narrow-minded, personal effort to hold me back.

Pop's "outside the locker room" talk convinced me to stay on the team. It set in motion events, lessons, relationships, and opportunities that have touched almost every area of my life. His words really were gold for me.

My father passed away in 2000. I'm still processing everything he stood for and said. I keep discovering how the things I say, think, and do can often be traced directly to him.

A couple of years ago, my sister sent me some of my parents' old stuff; it's amazing to look at. There are cancelled checks my dad wrote. His deteriorating handwriting on those checks records the way Parkinson's affected Pop. There's the receipt from the last car he bought. Those mundane, little relics of my dad's life are now precious to me.

In that collection are letters from his supervisors at the veterans' hospital, recognizing him for acts of kindness to the patients. There's his badge from the care center where he spent his last years—marked to show that he was both a patient *and* a volunteer. He never stopped affecting the people around him.

Some might have seen Parkinson's as a handicap that sidelined Dad from the action. But that's where coaches do their work. And my dad was a coach.

What's most special to me among these heirlooms are the notebooks where Dad scribbled his insights—kind of like Proverbs from Pop. I can still hear him speaking some of these words, and it reminds me of how much he invested himself in each of his children. Maybe that's why it's so easy for me to think of him as a coach.

Coaches are known for their one-liners. Pop's notebooks are filled with his.

Example: "I'm sure we all feel it's nice to be important, but it's more important to be nice." That may sound like a cliché, but such phrases mean something when they're backed up by a life.

In another place he wrote, "Be consistent in attitude." Still another page says, "Let's stop being overanxious."

Dad wasn't into making long speeches—leading me to wonder how I ended up being a public speaker—but he always said a lot in a few words. He was never a "do as I say, not as I do" kind of father. When he said it, he was doing it.

Then there's this line: "Family should be honest with each other." Books and doctoral dissertations have been written about family communication, but Pop summed up the issue in a sentence. On marriage, he wrote, "The wife contributes to the behavior of the husband, and the husband contributes to the behavior of the wife."

I don't know what was going on that made him write these things. I'd love to turn to him now and say, "I can see how this is true between me and my bride, Dad. How was it true for you and Mom?"

Or how about this gem? "Don't argue with confused people." I want to remember that next time I run into someone who clearly doesn't know what he's talking about but wants to defend it anyway.

I know these aren't revolutionary insights. But that was my Pop, my coach. His words still resonate and have power for me, and reading them brings a little bit of him back.

Just as I still benefit from my dad's wisdom, you can influence your children. Part of coaching your kids is speaking truth to them—consistently, at the right time. Some of it can be spoken, and my Pop did that a lot. But try writing notes, messages, and even journals for your children. Take Bible verses and other truths you hold dear and pass them on. Give your kids plenty to remember and think about—even after you're gone.

A Coach by Design

When it comes to pregnancy and birth, our wives definitely have done the heavy lifting. Conception may involve intense pleasure for both spouses, but the rest of the process usually requires discomfort, time, and pain. A dad's contribution to child creation is almost instantaneous; our wives' contribution is more like an epic! She gets the morning sickness, swollen ankles, sore back, let-down reflex, and stretch marks—not to mention the joys of delivery!

I don't want to go on and on about this, but a man who doesn't stand in absolute awe before what his wife has endured in bringing their children into the world still has a lot to learn about honor, humility, and love!

What does that have to do with coaching? It's part of the reason I'm convinced we dads were designed to coach our kids.

Mothers and fathers relate to children differently. Mom's connected in a way you can't be. That child started in her body as a combination of one large cell from her and one little cell from you. There was a physical cord between mother and baby; it had to be cut at birth.

That's why moms' feelings for their children are different from ours. Theirs are direct; ours are more distant. Your wife probably feels your children are an extension of her in a way that you don't.

That word I used—*distant*—can be a negative term. But I don't mean it that way. When it comes to fathers, I believe distance can be used for perspective, wisdom, and coaching. We are somewhat apart by design.

Often we dads struggle to bridge the distance, while moms may struggle to create some! But parenting is a team endeavor, and both moms and dads have crucial roles.

If you're a single parent, that poses a big challenge. It's important to arrange for the other-parent perspective to be represented in your child's life as much as possible. People who think they literally can be both mom and dad may end up doing neither role very well.

If you want a classic example of how distance works in parenting, try this. If your child is involved in a sport, take your wife to an event in which one of your kids is competing. Observe how the two of you experience the event. You're both watching your son or daughter, but usually your perspectives will be very different.

For your wife, it's probably all about the child. *Will my daughter get hurt? Will my son get along with his teammates?* She takes developments on the field personally.

Most of us dads, meanwhile, watch our son or daughter in the context of the game. We're shouting performance-oriented encouragement while, right next to us, our wives are shouting, "Be careful!" We watch our child fall down and urge him to get up and keep going—while we hold our wives back from running onto the field to hug him and see if he's really okay.

It's a matter of distance. And there is at least one very good reason why we dads were given the gift of distance from our kids: so we can coach them!

You need to provide a perspective for your children that complements what your wife brings to their lives. The original design is for our kids to get the very best from both of us! You can't mother your kids any more than you can volunteer to carry the next baby to term. We're different by design.

A lot of dads unconsciously use distance as an excuse to stay away from their kids. They think, *I've got a gap to bridge between me and my children, and it's going to take too much effort. I quit.*

Don't do it! Those kids of yours need you as a coach more than you can imagine on your best day. You've got a perspective they can't get anywhere else.

Papa, Don't Preach

Think of coaching as training your children—not preaching at them. Don't just fold your arms and say, "This is what I said to do." Instead, be involved; share insights and help your children work through the challenges of life.

Coaching changes as your kids mature into adults. The younger the child, the greater will be your direct control. But that will change as he or she grows. Your role will gradually shift from control to influence as your child develops personal independence and responsibility.

When Peyton Manning was a rookie quarterback, he had to do exactly what his coach told him to do. He had to develop an ability to carry out his coach's plans. Once Manning demonstrated that he could "see" the game, the coach gave him more and more freedom to call the game on the field.

We, too, want to prepare our children to make good decisions and practice wisdom. We're not always going to be there to do the choosing for them!

A well-known proverb from the Bible tells us, "Train a child in the way he should go, and when he is old he will not turn from it" (Proverbs 22:6). Training includes discipline and correction, but it's also sharing from our own experiences and practicing the principles. And it's taking into account each child's unique gifts, interests, challenges, and vulnerabilities.

One of the most powerful pictures of coaching can be found in the instructions God gave the people of Israel about passing on His commands to future generations: "These commandments that I give you today are to be upon your hearts. Impress them on your children. Talk about them when you sit at home and when you walk along the road, when you lie down and when you get up" (Deuteronomy 6:6-7).

The two big coaching ideas here are *persistence* and *pervasiveness*.

Persistence leads to repetition. A good coach knows when to repeat an instruction. Few of us learn after one hearing.

Pervasiveness comes from realizing that every day is filled with "coachable" moments. The locations may change, but the wisdom we need to convey to our children fits everywhere—at home or on the road, when winding down or getting up.

I can remember when my son Marcellus was a freshman in high school. He was all "buff"; he thought he was the man. Girls were chasing him down—coming to the house, calling on the phone.

We'd talked plenty of times about girls and sex and all that, but I knew it was time to take it to the next level. So I took him to the park; I wanted to talk plainly, and his sisters were in the house.

I said, "Son, the route you're going, this is what's going to happen," and I got very specific with him. Then I said, "Those girls don't have your best interests in mind, and the way they're coming to the house, the way they're dressed, I don't think their moms and dads are getting a chance to see them before they leave home.

"I want to shoot you straight: God made men and women to be attracted to each other. And Son, if you aren't careful and aware of what's happening, things are going to happen that will change your life forever. One of these girls could get you to give up a gift I know you want to save for the woman you're going to spend your life with. I don't want you to have any regrets on your wedding night."

I had to school him up—to coach him. That's my role as his father.

Some might say my approach was close to preaching. But the kind of preaching we need to avoid is the kind that ignores the uniqueness and feelings of the child we're talking to. When my dad would tell my brother and me, "Boys, let's take a drive," he'd talk respectfully to us in the car about sex, about drugs, about life. He didn't fold his arms and squint at us as if to say, "Boy, you're stupid."

We needed that coaching from our dad. And that's what your kids need from you.

The Challenge to Coaches

As with other aspects of Championship Fathering, our society isn't making it easy to coach these days.

Not long ago in Houston, a dad named Mitch was eating lunch in the airport with his five-year-old daughter. Their delightful moments together were interrupted when a police officer approached to question them. Apparently someone had observed them and reported their interactions to the authorities as "suspicious."

In Illinois, a dad received a call from the director of his son's day care center. She said someone had expressed concern because he was seen touching the children "inappropriately." What had he been doing? Volunteering to read stories to his son and several other kids—some of whom had sat on his lap as he read.

That's how things are today. In church preschool programs, men don't help kids use the bathroom. Parents are advised never to hire a male babysitter. Airlines avoid placing unaccompanied children next to male passengers.

We can understand how this has come about. A tiny percentage of men really are "bad guys," and they've changed things for the rest of us. Some dads even refuse to hold their own child's hand in public. But we have to find a way to "be there." Kids may read our caution as a form of rejection—and conclude that something's wrong with them.

Many fathers, of course, aren't just neglecting their role as coach; they're barely around at all. You've probably heard the statistics showing how father absence is linked to higher rates of poverty, failure in school, teen pregnancy, substance abuse, violent crime, depression, and ultimately a loss of hope. When we aren't coaching, our children can drift into dangerous waters.

I believe others can help fill the vacuum created by a father's absence, but denying the vacuum exists doesn't make it go away. The "fathering deficit" is a seriously ignored crisis in our culture.

When you take on your coaching role as part of the Championship

Fathering team, you'll be swimming against the current. But I know you don't want to see a world in which even more children grow up fatherless, and dads are regarded with even more suspicion and distrust. And you certainly don't want your kids to drift aimlessly in a world like that.

It's tougher than ever to be a close and caring dad. The pursuit of Championship Fathering is not going to be an easy goal to reach—but your children are definitely worth the effort.

It's time to take up the coaching challenge. The next chapter will help you do that. If I'm right, and you were designed to coach, your kids need the best you can give them. Since we've come this far together, I'm willing to count on the fact that you want to do what it takes to develop a coach's mind-set.

ACTION POINTS

How to Coach

Preschool
- Have your child join you in completing a household task, and find ways to make it fun.
- Be proactive in protecting your children. Talk them through wise responses to potentially dangerous situations—like crossing a busy street, dealing with strangers, and avoiding hazardous chemicals at home.
- When talking with your child, remember to get down on his or her level so you're more likely to speak conversationally.
- Use the power of imitation and repetition to teach your kids how to pick up their toys, fold socks, get dressed, etc. Let them watch you do it; then help them do it more than once.
- Let your children experience some negative consequences for poor choices. Don't *become* the consequence by screaming at them or otherwise putting them down.

- Work on making positive comments to your children. Focus on the good that you want from them instead of the negatives they need to avoid or have already done.

Elementary
- Teach your child a skill—tying a necktie, checking and inflating a car's tires, hanging a picture on the wall, etc.
- Revisit the topic of safety. For instance, talk about using appliances and electricity, protecting identity on the Internet, and proper and improper touches.
- Include at least one of your children when you run errands—and, if you can, take one on an occasional out-of-town business trip.
- Consider teaching your child's Sunday school class in order to see how your child and others learn.
- Start your children on a regular allowance and budget plan that helps them learn how to manage money.
- Talk to your kids about the value of self-discipline. Choose a day when everyone agrees to say "no" to something he or she would normally enjoy. Discuss results the next evening.
- Tell your children something positive you learned from your father.
- As you get involved in your child's education, give special attention to life skills, character development, and spiritual matters.
- Work with your child to establish a good homework routine; be available to help.
- Come up with questions that prod your child to really think or look up answers: "Why are manhole covers round?" "Why are nickels bigger than dimes?"

Teen
- Talk your kids through scenarios in which they could face tough decisions or peer pressure. Help them plan the right choices before they find themselves in those situations.

- Affirm qualities your teen has that would make him or her a good husband or wife.
- Be willing to share mistakes from your past without going into too much detail; talk honestly about negative consequences, pain, and lessons learned.
- Take your teen on a one-on-one dinner date or ice cream outing; focus on listening to his or her concerns.
- Have an informal talk with your son or daughter about relationships, letting him or her know how the opposite sex tends to think and react.
- Suggest three or four ways to say "No" when offered alcohol or other drugs. Give your kids permission to call you if they're ever in a risky situation. Promise that you'll come and get them—and not interrogate them when you get there.
- Read a short story, editorial, or magazine or newspaper article with your teen. Then ask his or her opinion.
- Give your child opportunities to gain experience with bank accounts, credit cards, and other financial tools on a small scale—while you're there to provide counsel.
- Do a practice job interview.
- Help your teen track how he uses his time for a week. Then check the results and discuss whether they reflect his goals and priorities.
- Schedule a time to get away for a few days with your teen. Plan both fun activities and relevant topics to discuss.

For additional practical tips on fathering, subscribe to the National Center for Fathering's free e-mail, *fathers.com weekly,* at www.fathers.com/weekly. You'll also find articles on a wide range of fathering situations and challenges at www.fathers.com.

CHAPTER EIGHT

Coaching with Insight

My Pop worked in a Veterans Administration hospital. But he thought of himself as a philosopher. He liked to lay profound thoughts on us kids, then observe as we tried to figure them out. I mentioned some of his "proverbs" in the last chapter.

One of his favorite words was "watch." He'd say, "Son, you must always *watch*."

The first time he did that, there was something in his tone that caught my attention. "C'mon, Pop," I said. "What do you mean, 'watch'? School me, Dad."

It turned out that "watch" was his way of saying, "Be careful. Don't take life lightly. Don't get hurt because you weren't paying attention to something important."

Usually we'd hear this when someone had gotten us in trouble. Pop would tell us, "Son, watch. Don't be in the wrong place at the wrong time and get your car shot at." Or, "Watch! Don't be at some party where you don't need to be. Watch!"

We also heard it when others made tragic mistakes. A young man in my hometown, one of the greatest athletes ever to come up, drowned in the river his senior year because he underestimated the currents. "Watch," Pop told us.

A few years later, my cousin took off in his car late one night to meet some girls, even after his father told him it wasn't a good idea. He missed a turn, and it ended his life. "He wasn't watching," my dad said.

Back then I got tired of hearing it. Today, though, I see the value of his speaking truth into my life. He saved me from difficult times and big regrets. Reminding me to "watch" was a form of coaching.

That kind of guidance has a way of becoming part of a family's fiber. I noticed that one day several years ago, when I visited my daughter Patrice at college. As I left her dorm room, I saw that word, boldly typed and taped above the doorknob: "Watch." She valued that word from my dad, and wanted to be reminded each time she walked out that door.

Like my Pop, you have lessons you've learned. How will you pass them on? By lecturing?

No. If you want to make sure your kids hear and remember what you believe and what you want for them, try the Championship Fathering way—by becoming an insightful coach.

What Coaches Do—and Don't

As I mentioned in the previous chapter, Moms are in a unique position to develop a close, nurturing relationship. We dads can't duplicate that, nor should we try. We were designed to offer something equally valuable to our children—perspective and protection.

To help us carry out our unique fathering function, this design creates a certain distance in our relationship. That distance gives us room to look, observe, reach conclusions, and offer wisdom. In short, we're meant to have a coach's insight into our children's lives.

I believe we dads have a unique opportunity to guide our children. But I'm afraid we don't take hold of that opportunity as we should. We have the capacity to do it insightfully, but we don't use it enough.

We also tend to think coaching is just about dispensing advice. But that's not the first step. Effectively guiding our kids first requires observing them—and then taking the time to act on what we discover.

A good coach spends hours watching his players. He breaks down their skills and can describe in great detail their positive and negative habits. He knows their tendencies, usually better than the players themselves do. A truly attentive coach can identify a player just by seeing his footwork.

Everything a coach learns about his players goes into designing strategy and deciding how to use that player to the greatest advantage. We dads need to know our kids in a similar way. The more we know our children, the better we'll be able to guide their steps.

I've seen this illustrated countless times in my own family. Recently, for instance, the subject came up when I watched Chance play basketball.

Seeing Chance play is a real adventure. He may not be the most gifted or motivated basketball player in the world (though he *was* born on Michael Jordan's birthday in Chicago). But he's learning the game and enjoying being part of a team.

During this particular contest, he was assigned to guard a player man-on-man. Let me tell you, Chance was all over that boy! The poor kid could barely breathe, let alone get a pass. My boy was doing the job.

On offense, Chance wasn't getting many opportunities. But whenever he did get the ball, you know what I was yelling:

"Shoot it, Son!"

"Go to the hole!"

"Chuck it up there!"

"Slam dunk!"

Did I mention that dads tend toward performance-based cheering?

I learned something that day. There was Chance, holding the ball and hearing all those voices. The other players were slapping at the ball. What did he do? He did what his coach had taught him. He looked for a teammate, spotted the open man, and made a pass that led to an easy layup.

After the game, I listened as the coach gave awards to team members— most points, most rebounds, that type of thing. My son got the award for sportsmanship.

I've always thought it would be great if my kids could be leaders and high achievers on the playing fields—and in other areas of life. But that day I was reminded that God created my son the way he is. The Lord has plans for my boy—plans to prosper him, to provide hope and a future (see Jeremiah 29:11). I'd say being a good sport and a good teammate is a solid place to start.

I'll continue to cheer Chance on with great enthusiasm. But it isn't my job to press him into being someone else. I'm seeing more and more that my children will do much better if their heavenly Father is leading and guiding them—and their earthly one is just assisting.

Gathering Insight

Almost any situation in which you observe your child can help you better understand his or her character, skills, and uniqueness. The more you know about your kids, the better.

And I'm talking *specifics*. Our research at the National Center for Fathering has consistently found that the most effective dads *pursue specific knowledge of their children*. Insight-based direction always works better than guessing what your kids need from you.

So how can you gather insights about your children? Try keeping a notebook about each child. Record your observations. Keep an updated list of their gifts and talents. Note memorable statements they make, and lessons they learn on their own. Track and date their achievements. Invite them to tell you what they think you need to know about them. The fact that you're paying attention will mean a lot to them.

When preparing for significant events like birthdays, consult your notebook. Be ready to comment on how you've noticed that child grow in the past year. No matter how old your children get, they'll always benefit from hearing wise insights about them from you. There's an amazing passage in Genesis 49 that describes Jacob as a very old man speaking words of blessing and insight to each of his 12 sons. The power of your thoughtful words will not diminish over time if they're true and loving.

Another way to gain insight into your children is to pray for them. Talk to God about them individually. You may be amazed at the thoughts that occur to you as you converse with the heavenly Father about your role as an earthly father. Since God designed each of your children, it makes sense to consult the One who really knows them, doesn't it?

Gaining insight into each of your kids helps you customize your approach to coaching, too. I remember what my dad did when I turned 16. I got my driver's license, but Pop wouldn't let me drive by myself for three months! I was not a happy camper. I protested: "But, Dad, I have my license! I passed the test! I'm the man! I'm street-legal. I can do this!"

But my daddy knew me. Years later—still traumatized by this "abuse" I'd suffered—I asked him about this.

"Son," he said, "I knew you would've gotten with Greg and Teddy and Cedric and the guys. Y'all would have piled in your car, and they would have been telling you, 'Hey, Carey, try to go 60! Try to go 70!' You would have been influenced by them, Son."

He'd made the right call. After I'd waited those three months, a lot of the thrill and newness of driving had passed. I'd gotten used to it, and everyone knew I could drive, so it was no big deal. The temptation to show off behind the wheel had been greatly reduced.

My dad's explanation reminded me of a constant in my childhood: He knew me. He knew my friends. He knew what I could and couldn't handle. I don't recall that he spent much time trying to explain exactly why he was delaying my privileges; he knew I wouldn't understand. He had to make the call whether I understood or not. That's what insightful coaches can do.

How well do you know your children's strengths and weaknesses? How would you describe their typical day? How do they prefer to spend their time? Do you know their best friends? What encourages and motivates them? What things embarrass them or hurt their feelings? Have they had any recent disappointments?

And how are you using your insights into their character to determine the way you father them?

That kind of specific awareness will help you protect your children. That's what my Pop did, and it's one of your most important jobs.

Insights Are Individual

If you have more than one child, do you treat them as individuals? Understanding one won't necessarily mean you understand them all!

Part of your coaching role is to look for ways in which your children differ from each other. You can use that specific knowledge to encourage, challenge, and even discipline them.

My older son, Marcellus, is a father himself now. But I can remember many times when I had to take drastic measures to get through to him on some important points, teaching him to be respectful and considerate of others—usually his sisters.

I'd give him a little punch in the arm to get his attention, and say, "Come here, Boy. Let me school you up." I can remember when Homeboy slammed my car door in anger, and we had a good, long discussion about self-control. "I understand anger, Son," I remember saying. "But a man stays in control, even when he's angry."

Often we went to the park to have these conversations, away from his sisters. There I could be more direct, talking man-to-man—kind of like the way my football coaches used to talk to me, only without the cursing. I really let him know what day it was, so to speak.

Then there's my younger son, Chance—14 years younger. I've changed a lot since Marcellus was a boy, but Chance isn't the same person his brother was, either. Chance gets into plenty of trouble, too, and needs my guidance and correction; but if I so much as raise my voice or look at him a certain way, it breaks his heart and he's just about ready to cry.

The differences are amazing, and I have to take them into account. I'm not sure I understood this as I should have with my older children. But now I'm really focusing on how Chance is unique and how I can best meet his needs.

At the same time, I can see how Marcellus's temperament is an advantage in his life and ministry. Perhaps God will use Chance for a calling that's completely different.

As we strive to be part of the Championship Fathering team, let's zero in on our children's strengths and weaknesses—what motivates, embarrasses, encourages, and hurts each of them. As they grow, and their personalities are shaped by friends and activities, their lives become more complex. So does the task of keeping up with them.

Insight in the Mirror

One of the benefits of seeking insight for coaching is that you end up learning a lot about yourself. Clarifying your kid's character almost always involves clarifying your own.

Your child is unique—but so are you, and knowing yourself as a father is just as important as knowing your child. Just as you'll never get to the end of learning about your children, you'll never reach the end of lessons about yourself.

My oldest daughter, Christie, is an adult. She's making her way in the world, finding her career path. God is already using her in some very special ways.

But not long ago, I heard her say, "It's tough being a Casey."

At first I thought, *Where does she get off complaining about her family?*

But then her words made sense. The sobering part was that, until that moment, I hadn't realized the pressure she was feeling. She wasn't rejecting it, just acknowledging it. I listened as she told me how she felt the need to perform a certain way, or win at whatever she tried, to avoid feeling she'd failed.

I can see where she's coming from. I'm not famous, but through the years I suppose I've gained visibility in some circles. Our family has connections with a wide range of people around the country. So I can understand if she feels there's a reputation to live up to. It probably doesn't help that in my current position I'm regularly talking and writing about her and her siblings, either.

Christie and I had a long talk about how proud I am of her and always will be. I told her I love her unconditionally.

I hope that will take some of the pressure off. Now I'm thinking I need to have the same conversation with Chance.

Consider your own kids. Are they feeling pressure to carry on the family business, attend a particular college, perform in the arts, excel at sports, or continue in some pursuit because it's your thing? Give them some breathing room.

It can be good for our kids to know we have high expectations. But it's up to you to be aware of what your child is going through as a result. You may want to come right out and ask, "Do you feel pressure to be a certain way because you're my son or daughter?" or, "Am I putting expectations on you that aren't realistic?" You could even ask, "What is hard for you about being part of this family?"

Questions like these can multiply your insights about your children—and about how they see you.

Some Inconvenient Truths

Because our children are human, not everything we discover about them is going to be pleasant.

I'm sure it wasn't easy for Pop to acknowledge that as a 16-year-old I was still too easily influenced by my peers to be trusted alone with a car. It's sobering to face the fact that our child might lie too easily or have a problem with anger. Sometimes we even have to take the added step to get our kids special help.

As you observe your child, it's important to pay attention if you sense a change in him or her. Behavior changes provide clues we can't ignore, even though it's tempting to leave it at, "It's just a phase."

One father I know noticed that his daughter was increasingly anxious about being perfect, trying hard to do everything right. Her compulsion was gradually leading her to erratic behavior.

He and his wife talked it over; they decided that their gentle questions weren't revealing the problem. With the help of a caring counselor, they eventually discovered that their daughter had been molested several years earlier. She'd been dealing with her deep sense of shame and damage by frantically trying to be perfect in every other way.

It took outside assistance for those parents to gain enough insight to help her. But the process got started by noticing something wasn't quite right.

Other situations may be less traumatic, but still require our caring attention. Not long ago, Melanie and I came face-to-face with the difficult truth that our son has a mild learning challenge. It isn't a major disability, but it set me back for a while.

I knew our family wasn't perfect. But this seemed like the kind of thing that didn't happen to us. My three other children have their strengths and weaknesses, but they didn't have this specific challenge.

I started asking the questions I'm sure are normal in these kinds of situations: *What caused this? Was it something I did—or didn't do? Did we miss something that could have made a difference?*

It wasn't long before those more self-centered thoughts turned to love and concern for my son. No matter what had happened in the past, what could I do now to help him?

Hey, I told myself, *this is my time to step up. I have to be a father. I need to be there for my son.* And that's the way it is, even if the insights we gain by observing our kids tell us things we're reluctant to hear.

Championship Checklist

The following statements have helped many fathers identify the insights they need to develop in order to coach their children. As you come up with a profile for each of your kids, try substituting their names when the words "my child" are used here.

1. *I know what encourages my child.* Do you understand how to keep your child going, and how to enter into his or her times of disappointment and discouragement? Your confidence in this area will grow with trial and error.

Some kids want to talk it out while you listen; others want to think it out while you wait with them. Your child may want to hear you say what he or she has a hard time believing: "You can do it! You can keep going."

All kids need encouragement. The challenge is that each child has his or her own "encouragement code" that you must keep working to decipher.

2. *I know what motivates my child.* Have you identified your child's "go buttons"? Most kids respond to rewards, though these vary from candy to cash to verbal praise. Sometimes competition is a motivator; many kids like the idea of "taking it up a notch." If the latter is true for your child, try saying something like, "This is how you did in the past; I think you can do it faster and better this time!"

3. *I know how my child's emotional needs change over time.* Kids often feel a tension between the security of dependence and the thrill of independence. Their experiences—failure to fit in at school, bullies, and any number of physical changes—provoke a wide range of feelings.

Adolescence—particularly with daughters—can be a bewildering roller coaster of emotions for a dad. Children need to know that what they feel or experience won't change the fact that we love them.

4. *I know my child's gifts and talents.* Identify and celebrate the ways in which each of your children is unique. If you have several children who display similar talents (they're all musically inclined, for example), make sure you note how they're distinct. Look for the subtle differences that make each child God's unique creation, and which offer something very special to the world.

5. *I know my child's growth needs.* This may require you to do a little reading and ask some questions. Your child's teacher may be an excellent source of insight. Pay attention to transitions and how they will affect your child: home to school; elementary to middle school; middle school to high school. These changes may seem automatic, but can cause a lot of trauma in kids' lives.

6. *I know what my child needs to grow into a mature adult.* How are you preparing your children for independence? Do you allow them to experience a sequence of "supervised responsibilities" and "limited freedoms" that help

them develop? Responsibility can't be learned simply through explanation; it has to be experienced. Simple chores and shared duties are small steps toward independence.

7. *I know the issues with which my child is dealing.* Participating in our children's lives needs to be accompanied by reflection.

What can you learn from watching how your son or daughter functions as a member of the basketball team? It's more than observing how he or she plays; it's noting what he or she does when *not* playing.

How do your kids relate to their teammates? Are they encouraging others? Are they "in the game" even when they're not on the field? Can you say something like, "I noticed how you went over and sat with that kid who really messed up on the play; I know that would have meant a lot to me if I were that kid"?

This will also involve asking your children gentle, probing questions and listening carefully to their answers. If we demonstrate from their earliest days that we're deeply interested in their experiences, they'll give us glimpses into their lives as they grow.

Using these seven research-based statements can help you gauge the level of insight you have into each of your children. If this feels discouraging when you start, remember that you probably know more than you think; you just aren't used to thinking about what you see when you're with your kids.

To help you reflect, take an event like last Christmas and relive it by "watching" each of your kids in those moments. Did all of them approach the day the same way? How did each child handle gifts? How did each child deal with giving as well as receiving? You may be amazed at how many individual traits will emerge, and with them insights into how best to coach your kids.

Coaching and Discipline

Part of coaching your children is disciplining them. It's probably not your favorite part. But kids don't turn out well without direction, and they don't learn without correction. So let me offer a few suggestions.

1. *Discipline works best when Mom and Dad form a united front.* If the two of you can't agree on how to discipline, your kids will suffer the consequences. Make sure your discussions about discipline take place in private.

2. *Discipline is never an excuse to lose control and lash out with words or actions.* What your child did may make you very angry, but it shouldn't make you lose control. You're the adult; your son or daughter is the child. If he or she finds out it's possible to manipulate you by making you angry, you'll be forever tied up in emotional knots. To apply discipline, you must practice it.

3. *Don't make threats you won't carry out.* Children have an uncanny capacity for noting and remembering idle threats, even when those warnings are shouted. If kids know you won't keep your word when it comes to discipline, they'll disobey. The earlier in life they realize that you always do exactly what you say you will—calmly, even cheerfully if possible—the more secure they'll feel. Your kids want to know you'll stand by your word, even if it means they have to pay a penalty.

4. *Consistency is usually more important than the mode of discipline.* It confuses children when we're all over the place—warning 10 times once and once the next time, promising punishment and forgetting about it, or letting fatigue or fury dictate our actions instead of enforcing a clear set of reasonable rules.

Discipline is one part of coaching that can't be done by remote control. In fact, it's a good idea to stay close enough to your kids that they get the impression you might show up at any time to dispense justice.

One dad, Gerry, knew his son, Scott, was prone to get into trouble at school. The boy's impulsiveness sometimes caused problems in the classroom. As a good coach, Gerry wanted Scott to learn to think before speaking or acting.

Gerry, a baker, talked with Scott's teacher in front of his son. "If Scott causes you any problems," Gerry said, "I want you to call me at work. I will stop kneading the dough and baking my loaves and I will come down here covered with flour and help you deal with my son."

In Scott's mind, the image of his father showing up in a cloud of flour was a potent picture. It was enough to keep Scott out of trouble!

No doubt it helped that Gerry wasn't just interested in showing up as an avenging angel. He was a loving dad, committed to be involved in his son's life. The proof: Scott was also a great athlete, and Gerry showed up flour-free for his events!

One way or another, we want our children to be confident that when they need our coaching—even if they don't always want it—we'll be there.

Learning from the Greats

Do you have a child who faces a major challenge like autism, Down's syndrome, cancer, or the scarring of burns? Dads like you often set the bar high and help the rest of us define what it means to be a committed, insightful coach—and a Championship Father.

When the needs of your child have required extra sacrifices, you've probably stepped up. You've put your child's needs before your own and never regretted it. I realize you haven't done this to be recognized, but I want to recognize you as a great example to other dads.

The rest of us would do well to take a page from your playbook. We need to make radical decisions to sacrifice our own desires and goals for the sake of our children. No matter what those children's gifts, abilities, and weaknesses may be, we need to cherish them for who they are.

If we do that, they can teach us what it means to be committed fathers and insightful coaches. You don't have to be everybody's father, after all—just a dad who keeps a growing collection of insights to inform the way you coach your particular kids.

One of my heroes is Tony Dungy, coach of the Super Bowl champion Indianapolis Colts. When his book *Quiet Strength* came out, I devoured it—not just because Tony is a friend, but also because he's been a great example to me of fathering under pressure. The stresses of his position in the spotlight of professional football and the challenges he's had to face in his personal life have made me appreciate him all the more. Tony exemplifies what it means to be open and transparent as a father and coach in the midst of a high-pressure life.

When They Start to Coach You

A coach holds his players accountable. A father does the same. And when they get old enough, our kids may do the same for us.

I've discovered some of the delights of this kind of accountability with my son Marcellus, who's in his twenties. During weekly phone calls, we ask each other hard questions about our thought lives, integrity at work, stewardship, and more.

We have a regular appointment. Usually he's at home, but when he's on the road I know it's even more important. I'll ask him things like, "Son, who are you rooming with at the hotel? What are you doing with your free time?"

This process started a bit unexpectedly, back when Marcellus was in college. One evening I had a speaking engagement, and he came along for the ride. After the event, as the two of us walked to the car, Marcellus said, "Dad, let me see your cards."

I said, "My cards? You've seen my business card."

"No, give me the cards you got tonight from other people."

I handed him the stack of cards. He went through them and pulled one out. "You won't be needing *this* one," he said.

"What're you talking about, Son?"

He said, "No, this lady does not have Mom's best interests in mind."

I looked at him, confused.

"No, Dad, I saw her. She got in your space." He pointed to the name on the card, and I remembered. She was a younger, single lady—very sharp, very attractive. "I know she could do a lot to help your organization," Marcellus added, "but you need to send somebody *else* to have lunch or meet with her."

I heard what he was saying, though I wasn't sure his suspicions were justified. But several months later I saw some pretty clear evidence that my son's hunch had been right on. He'd become a coach—and an insightful one. He was looking out for me as a man.

It's natural for us to think about coaching our kids by holding them accountable. But we need this from them, too. Can you give your older children permission to ask you about anything—and be willing to give an honest answer? Can you open up about some of your struggles and mistakes? Ask them to pray for you in a particular area?

As our children mature, they and we benefit from being more transparent and vulnerable. We need each other's insightful coaching.

It's About Time

Our child-rearing years may seem to pass in slow motion at times. But when we look back at them, they seem quick as a breath.

We tend to think of time as a fluid thing—that we've got plenty of it. But we can't insist that our kids stay young until we get around to doing all that insightful coaching we planned to do for them. If we miss that time, we miss it.

I'm not writing this to make you feel bad about the times you may have already missed in your kids' development. I'm doing it to encourage you not to miss any more.

To use a word Pop used so effectively: *Watch.*

Don't let the seasons of your children's lives keep rolling by while you think about "someday." I hope you'll put on your "Coach Dad" hat—and never take it off again.

 ACTION POINTS

How to Coach with Insight

Preschool

- Talk with your child's mother about your child's development and in what areas you need to be more involved during the next six months.

- Form the habit of writing short letters to your child about milestones in his or her development and what you're experiencing as a father. Plan to give your child these letters at some point when he or she is older.
- Interview your child as if you haven't seen him in years, showing keen interest in his responses.
- Go to the library or online and read up on the developmental needs of your child.
- Before giving your child instructions, focus on understanding what motivates, embarrasses, encourages, and hurts him or her.

Elementary
- Check in regularly with your children's teachers, coaches, and youth sponsors to make sure they're doing well developmentally and socially.
- Have your child explain some of his or her homework to you. Ask questions to keep drawing out what he or she knows.
- Check out your child's favorite TV program, recording artist, Web site, or video game. Seek to understand why it appeals to him or her.
- Attend your child's sports practice, music lesson, or class at school. Your goal: gaining insight into his or her identity and way of thinking.
- What's your child's learning style? If you don't know, find out. One helpful resource is *Talkers, Watchers, and Doers* by Cheri Fuller (Piñon Press, 2004). Knowing your child's learning style is a great way to discover his or her unique needs.
- Observe your children in their "natural" habitats—for example, when they arrive at school and begin interacting with friends. (Don't try to deceive them, though, by hiding and "spying" on them.)
- Contact your child's teachers—especially the new ones—to ask, "How is my child doing?" "What do you notice about him so far?" And, "What can I do to help?"

- Engage your child in conversation and really listen. Say, "Let's make sure I understand. Do you mean . . . ?"
- Hang out in the vicinity of your children when they return from school or elsewhere; wait until they decide to start talking about their day. Having food nearby might help keep them there.

Teen

- Ask your child to tell you the three best qualities of his or her best friend, or of the love interest in his or her life.
- Seek wise counsel from other dads who've been through a situation you're likely to face with your children soon.
- Ask your child to name two privileges he's looking forward to, and help him develop a plan to earn them if they're suitable for his age.
- Volunteer to host or chaperone an event for your teen's church youth group.
- Tell your children what you thought of your dad when you were a teenager, and how that changed when you became an adult.
- Be aware of how you talk about your work at home. Does it come across as a grind or a calling? Do you mostly complain about your job, or do you talk about people you've helped or lessons you've learned? Remember, many of your child's notions about the world of work will come from your attitudes.
- Sign up with your child for a sport, hobby, or service project that he or she is likely to enjoy.
- As my father did, encourage your children to "watch." Talk to them about foolish mistakes some people make, perhaps using examples from the news.

For additional practical tips on fathering, subscribe to the National Center for Fathering's free e-mail, *fathers.com weekly,* at www.fathers.com/weekly. You'll also find articles on a wide range of fathering situations and challenges at www.fathers.com.

Modeling

You never know what your kids might imitate about you. Sometimes it's tragic. Sometimes, though, it's pretty funny.

I've seen it in my family. It started long before I became a father.

My Pop was a blessing, but he wasn't perfect. When I was a teenager, there were times I thought he was weird. He looked like El Nerdo, with his pants hitched up to his belly button. I kept telling him, "Pop, it ain't working. You gotta sag those pants a little bit." He would just smile and go about his business.

I'm here to tell you, the shoes I wear and the way I dress today . . . are just like Pop. That's right! Now, *I'm* El Nerdo with my pants pulled up.

My kids, of course, have always thought it was their duty to point out my fashion *faux pas*. Especially my son Marcellus. In his teens, he told me, "Dad, man, don't make Chance pull his pants up like that. He's gonna go to school and get beat up." He laid it on thick. But I took a clue from Pop and just smiled.

As Marcellus got a little older, though, I would sometimes come home from traveling and find shoes or shirts missing from my closet—"permanently borrowed." Then, not long ago, I saw a video of 24-year-old Marcellus performing his first wedding. There was something peculiar about his pants.

That's right—they were hitched up high. He'd become El Nerdo, just like his dad.

Fortunately, there's nothing in Championship Fathering that specifies how high you can wear your pants! But it's important to understand our kids' tendency to imitate us—whether we want them to or not. Modeling is making the most of that tendency for our children's benefit.

The Meaning of Modeling

In the last two chapters, we looked at coaching—standing on the sidelines and talking, whispering in our kids' ears, shouting from the stands, urging them on with wisdom, counsel, guidance, and correction. When we're coaches, our children are the ones doing, playing the game of life.

Modeling is different. When we're models, we're the players; our children learn by copying our moves.

Modeling starts early. Kids are watching and taking cues from us even before they can tell us what they see. We can't live in their place or make their choices for them, but what we do and say in front of them can shape their lives.

As with loving and coaching, we're modeling every day. The issue you and I have to resolve is, "What kind of model will I be?"

It can be scary to hear your toddler use a tone that you know he or she picked up from you. And have you ever heard your child say a word you use all the time—but which suddenly doesn't sound that appropriate?

Kids are natural-born imitators. They copy the way we walk and talk. That's why you've never heard a toddler raised in the Deep South say his first words with a New England accent. Modeling goes on in your home every moment of every day.

Of the three fundamental aspects of Championship Fathering (loving, coaching, and modeling), this one seems most out of our control. We don't get to decide what our children pick up from us and what they reject. They get to choose.

This is the scariest part of parenting. We can try to do everything right and our kids still turn out wrong. We can model; we can't mold. The older they get, the more we realize that they'll live their own lives.

So is modeling a wasted effort? Absolutely not. Without positive, intentional modeling, we don't even give our children a *chance* to imitate the good stuff!

Models with Feet of Clay

Unfortunately, our modeling isn't always positive or intentional. If you want an example of a dad who didn't practice what he preached, look no further than King Solomon in the Bible. He's a stunning specimen of a man who had the credentials to be an ideal father—but a track record of dismal failure when it came to actually fathering.

Solomon collected fatherly wisdom; the entire book of Proverbs is written from the point of view of a dad giving insight to his son. So Solomon's son Rehoboam may have gotten an earful of Dad's advice. But he didn't really *get* it. Why? Because he didn't see Dad live it.

Here's how the biblical record describes Solomon's behavior:

> King Solomon, however, loved many foreign women besides
> Pharoah's daughter. . . . They were from nations about which the
> Lord had told the Israelites, "You must not intermarry with them,
> because they will surely turn your hearts after their gods." Neverthe-
> less, Solomon held fast to them in love. He had seven hundred wives
> of royal birth and three hundred concubines, and his wives led him
> astray. As Solomon grew old, his wives turned his heart after other
> gods, and his heart was not fully devoted to the Lord his God, as the
> heart of David his father had been. . . . So Solomon did evil in the
> eyes of the LORD; he did not follow the Lord completely, as David
> his father had done. (1 Kings 11:1-4, 6)

When Rehoboam took over the throne from his father (1 Kings 12), he had an important choice to make: Would he reign like his father, or like his father *should* have reigned? Rehoboam got wise input from others; but in the end, his father's example was louder than anyone's words. The son squandered an amazing heritage because his dad left him the legacy of a poor model.

The stakes were huge, but Rehoboam made the wrong decision: to oppress the Israelites even more than his father had. Solomon set up his own son for failure.

Negative modeling happens a lot these days as well. The results are often disastrous, even when people recognize they've been watching a bad example.

Few children raised by an alcoholic parent say, "I can't wait to grow up so that I can be an alcoholic, too." Usually, they declare just the opposite: "I'll *never* drink like my dad; my life is not going to be anything like my parents' lives." Few people survive an abusive childhood and say, "I was glad to get out of the house so I could start abusing my own children." Yet research shows that children who grow up in these obviously destructive environments often grow up to repeat the experience. Why?

Part of the explanation is that focusing on what we *don't* want to be doesn't give us a clue about what we *do* want to be. The negative model, the only one the child really knows, becomes the default. It's like driving away at high speed from an accident while staring at the scene in our rearview mirror. We end up replicating the tragedy.

Out with the Bad, In with the Good

You may be thinking right now about your own upbringing. Maybe there were things about your dad that you didn't want to copy, but they've become very much a part of your life. What can you do?

The answer is that recognizing a negative model is an important step, but not the journey. If you say, "I don't want to be like my dad in *this* way," that's a realization—not a goal or objective. You have to finish the thought by saying, "This is who I *do* want to be like in *this* way."

It's not enough to turn away from a bad example; we have to turn toward a good one! Jesus applied that principle when He said this:

"When an evil spirit comes out of a man, it goes through arid places seeking rest and does not find it. Then it says, 'I will return to the house I left.' When it arrives, it finds the house unoccupied, swept clean and put in order. Then it goes and takes with it seven other spirits more wicked than itself, and they go in and live there. And the final condition of that man is worse than the first. That is how it will be with this wicked generation." (Matthew 12:43-45)

Whether we're talking about evil spirits, bad habits, or poor models, Jesus' picture holds true. It's not enough to say "out with the bad." That just creates an empty space. Whatever is wrong or unacceptable needs to be replaced with what's good and right.

Who are the fathers you want to be like? Find a person who demonstrates a trait you want to develop.

Every day I realize more what a great gift I have in a father who was such a positive model to me. There are few ways in which I wouldn't want to be like my dad. But I've always got my eyes open for other good models, knowing there are issues I face that my dad never had to deal with.

In a similar way, since our children have different skills and interests, we can't assume we'll be the ideal models for them in every area. But we can steer them to other coaches and mentors when necessary.

Ten Keys to Effective Modeling

Even though we aren't the only models our kids need, we're the primary ones. How do we take on that role?

Here are 10 ways in which we can improve our modeling as fathers.

Key #1: Aim for Consistency

You've probably heard the phrase, "More is caught than taught." We can try until we're blue in the face to explain away a bad behavior in ourselves, but our kids will invariably end up remembering and often copying what we did. The way they "catch" things is amazing—and frightening.

Wouldn't it be nice if we could edit our lives and show our kids only what we want them to see? But it wouldn't be real. Our children don't need a partial dad to use as a life pattern; they need a whole one.

We can't be certain what our children will choose to emulate. Their power to imitate some things about us and ignore others can be frustrating, but we can't let that take us out of our game plan.

Here's one way in which I deal with the uncertainty. Since I don't know what my kids will "catch" from my life, I try my best to eliminate and avoid anything I wouldn't want to pass on to my children. I never want to be in a situation that would be hard to explain if they showed up. I can't control their choices, but mine I can do something about!

I may not always hit that target. But I'm aiming for consistency, and so can you. To help us do that, we need to pay attention to what our kids are picking up from us and make corrections where we can.

Key #2: Try for Patterns, Not Perfection

If I try to be the perfect dad, I'm going to fail on a regular basis. But if I concentrate on establishing patterns in my life, those repeated exposures are going to have a bigger impact and create more lasting memories in my children's lives than the times here and there when I messed up.

I've already mentioned that my Pop wasn't perfect. But the patterns in his life made a big impression on me.

Dad was a devoted family man, a dedicated worker. He set a great example when it came to self-discipline and personal responsibility. I'll always remember how, when a big snowstorm was moving in, he'd plan accordingly the night before. He'd get up early to allow extra time to dig his car out or walk to work.

Another pattern he established was being involved with current events. He was patriotic and loved his country; since he was African American, that didn't seem very common to me. But he was "God bless America" more than most people. I didn't hear him put down the president. He believed our government had authority set up by God, and wanted to be obedient.

One of the most important patterns my dad adopted was modeling a strong commitment to my mother. Some of his friends divorced, and I know he and my mom struggled at times. But they respected each other, and that showed through. They made a decision to be there for one another, no matter what. As a result, there's no way I'm going to go off and do something foolish to damage my marriage or family. The pattern I saw in my father became deeply ingrained in me.

It doesn't always take much to establish a pattern your kids will remember. Someday you'll remember a handful of special times you did something with them— but to listen to them reminisce, it may sound like it happened every week.

One young father who enjoyed cross-country skiing didn't want to leave his sons behind. So he took them one at time, tucked them in a large backpack, and hit the trails. The kids loved the view and being with Dad. This wasn't exactly a regular event, but those two boys seem to think they spent most of their childhood winters snuggled in Dad's backpack!

Key #3: Take a Long-term View

Sometimes, in the heat of the moment, we blow a modeling opportunity. We get impatient or distracted or mad, forgetting the long-range effects it could have.

One dad faced this problem on trips with his kids. They repeatedly asked him, "When are we getting there?" or "Are we there yet?"

He realized they were pretty normal in that way. It was tiresome, but he didn't want to get into a pattern of expressing irritation or anger when they asked him those questions over and over.

So he decided to always answer the same way: "We'll be there in 12 days!"

He said it joyfully, as if it were the best news in the world. If they were going to pester him with predictable questions, he would respond with a predictable and self-controlled answer.

Once his kids caught on, they would sometimes counter with, "When are we getting there? And don't tell me 'in 12 days'!"

His backup response became, "Listen carefully to the sounds of the tires, kids. Every time those wheels go around, we get a little bit closer to being there."

Fast-forward 20 years. Those kids are now parents of children who are beginning to ask, "Are we there yet?" The "12-day" phrase is being introduced to a new generation. That father, now a grandfather, laughs out loud every time he hears it!

My dad also took a long-term approach to getting our family to church on time. He didn't stand over us and berate us for taking our time on Sunday mornings. He didn't work himself into a lather trying to speed us up. He simply made it clear that he was leaving at a certain time and expected us to plan ahead in order to be ready when that moment came.

When it did, he left the house in good spirits and went to church. We were accountable to the departure moment, not to continual checking on us.

By the time we were teenagers, we knew that if we weren't in the car on time, we'd be left behind. We also could expect an uncomfortable confrontation later—which is why we were seldom late, and why my memories of Sunday mornings are relatively peaceful ones.

Key #4: Don't Preach a Sermon, Be One

One of the biggest eye-openers in my life as a father happened when I was a young dad and pastor. My oldest child, Christie, was five; Patrice was three. It was Father's Day, and we were all getting ready for church.

I was in the living room, writing final notes for my Father's Day sermon. Christie knew it was a regular Sunday ritual for me to look over what I was going to preach. Running up and leaping on my lap, she asked, "Daddy, are you going to be a sermon today?"

She didn't mean it the way it came out. But I believe God speaks to us in mysterious ways, and He often uses the simple but powerful voices of our children.

That question became my sermon that morning—and has stayed with me ever since. I'll go to my grave remembering it.

It's a question I have to live up to every day. How about you? When you get down to it, are you modeling what you know is right, or just talking about it? Are you loving your children's mother? Are you really listening to your son or daughter? Is your life made up of patterns you'd be pleased for your kids to follow?

I'm finding it's much more important to my children that I *be* a sermon for them than preach one to them. We can *tell* our kids all day long how to live, but they're more likely to *do* what they see lived out day after day.

Key #5: When You Fail, Admit It

If you're a football fan, you might remember an incident that occurred during the 2006 season that got a lot of negative attention. Albert Haynesworth, a defensive lineman for the Tennessee Titans, lost control on the field. He lashed out at an opposing player in a cruel, despicable way. I won't repeat the details here.

Haynesworth was suspended, and in later interviews expressed deep remorse over his actions. One of the most powerful things he said contains a message for all of us fathers.

He apologized to his teammates, the opposing team, and the fans; but the biggest reason he admitted he had such deep regrets about that incident is because of the bad example he set for his children. "I am a father. . . . For a father to do something like that and for your kids to look up to you, I think is something very serious. . . . I have to keep doing the right thing."[1]

I wish he had taken a stand for the importance of being a role model for his children *without* the cruel act and the suspension. But the big lesson here for fathers is this: Sometimes we lose our cool and do things we later regret.

Being role models for our children should motivate us to be humble and transparent when we've messed up. It should also move us to watch our words and actions in the first place.

Most of us don't find our shortcomings broadcast around the world and repeated on sports highlights shows. Even if Haynesworth's story was a one-time event, the video of it will be played for years to come. His children may be asked about it repeatedly, and they may even be judged in some way by what their father did during a game.

Replays and questions can appear in our kids' minds, too—so watch your step. And when you mess up, be willing to confess your mistakes in a way that helps your children learn right along with you.

Key #6: Make a Sacrifice They'll Remember

Do you have a fond memory of a time when your dad modeled what a father should be by going the extra mile for you? Even if you don't, would you like your child to remember you that way?

When I think about my dad, one word that comes to mind is *unselfish*. He was a good steward of what he had, which wasn't a lot. He tithed faithfully, and was generous in ways we didn't fully appreciate at the time.

Maybe the best example of this came one fall when my brother and I were headed back to college. We couldn't afford to fly, so I was planning to take the car Pop had bought me for $400. It was a '64 Skylark, with three speeds on the column.

But then Pop said we could take *his* car to college—a brand-new Pontiac Catalina. Meanwhile, he would drive the Skylark.

That couldn't have been easy, being seen around town in my car. It had to be a humbling experience, not to mention the fact that he had to trust us with his vehicle. Maybe he was being practical, thinking it would be easier if we had the car that was less likely to break down. But still—how many fathers would send the family's best car to college with a child? It was an act of unselfish kindness.

But that's what dads do. They wear old shoes for a few more months so their kids can have a new pair. They pass up a second helping at dinner so their growing teenagers can eat it. They take a cold shower, saving the hot water for their kids, and squeeze the family budget to pay for their children's piano lessons, software, and catcher's mitts.

In so doing, they model the kind of character they hope their kids will have someday. The more memorable an act of selflessness, the more likely a child will be guided by it in the future.

That's worth remembering the next time your phone rings five minutes before curfew, in the middle of a thunderstorm, and your daughter says, "Dad, I ran out of gas!"

Key #7: Take Care What You Share
Admitting your weaknesses doesn't mean passing them on to your kids.

Recently I was talking with an NFL player, trying to help him through a tough time made worse by his drinking habit. I asked him, "Where did you first take a drink?"

"I drank a beer with my dad," he said.

Another young man I knew had been drinking when he got in an accident. All the other guys in the car either died or had serious injuries. This young man, who'd been driving, came out fine—though he served a short time in jail.

He came to me afterward to talk about it. I said, "Shoot me straight. When's the first time you ever took a drink?"

"With my dad," he replied.

Most dads would never intentionally initiate their children into a potentially destructive habit. But that's exactly what can happen if we let our guard down. If we're negative or inconsistent models, our kids may be vulnerable in that area, too.

We also need to be careful what we approve through silence or inaction. Does that TV show scene you just watched with your kids conflict with your values? Your children won't know that if you don't say it. You may need to use the mute button and talk about what happened on the screen. If you don't, it's reasonable for your kids to assume you're indifferent.

Key #8: Don't Make Promises You Can't Keep

When kids look up to you as a role model, broken promises are a big deal.

Remember the promises your father made? Do you remember more vividly those that were kept or those that were broken?

A lot of people have clear and painful memories of looking forward to a promised outing like a day fishing with Dad, or going to a ball game, or getting a certain birthday gift. Little did they know that Dad had completely forgotten the promise almost as soon as he made it.

To him it was a thought, a possibility. But they heard it as a certainty, and years later still remember the disappointment with a pang.

If a memory like this is holding you back, I encourage you to take the healthiest step possible and forgive that past disappointment. If you've failed to follow through on any promises (if you're not sure, ask your kids), get ready to apologize and make things right if you can. Then make sure you don't make casual promises from now on!

We role models are a lot like Superman in our younger kids' eyes—except that most of us don't wear the red and blue long underwear. They actually think there's nothing we can't do. So when we make promises, they take our words to the bank—and to heart.

It's easy to get into a pattern of broken promises and vague postponements ("I'm sorry Daddy couldn't be there, but I promise I'll be there some other time"). Our kids need to know that we keep our word—even to them.

Key #9: Use Everyday Events

The following was written by Brennan, a boy who's watching and learning from his father. You may or may not be smarter than a fifth-grader, but you can learn from this one.

Brennan contributed a winning entry in one of our Father of the Year Essay Contests. Here's what he wrote:

> When I talk to my dad, he never says "uh-huh" like some people do before you're even done talking. Dad really listens; he never criticizes me or yells at me.
>
> Dad holds the door open for women—this shows that he respects them. Mom never has to open any door when he's around or carry anything heavy. Dad says she works hard all day and if he can help her in any way, he will.
>
> Sometimes Dad and I will have a father-son day—this means we go to Home Depot and do "man things." We look at tools that we don't have any idea what they are used for and maybe one day we will buy them just to have them around just in case.
>
> When he gets really old, like 45 years old, I will be taking him on a father-son day and wheel him into Home Depot just to look around and touch things just like he used to do when I was just a kid.

Now, I don't really get that last comment about being old at 45. I guess it will take Brennan a few years to figure out that, as my Pop used to say, "You don't really get good until you're 50."

Other than that, I must commend this young man for noticing how well his father is modeling. Brennan's dad is using everyday events to set a good example of what it means to be a man and a father.

How? He's using routine conversations to show how to be quick to listen and slow to become angry. He's using doors and chores to model respect for women. He's using trips to Home Depot to demonstrate the interest in making things that so many dads would like to pass on to their kids.

Brennan's father is training him to be a man by letting the boy observe a man in action. That's a great lesson for you and me, as well as for that fifth-grader.

Key #10: Reinforce Actions with Words

Preaching without practicing is empty at best and hypocritical at worst. But that doesn't mean modeling can't involve talk. It doesn't have to be pantomime.

I'm reminded of the example of a man I greatly respect—Dr. Samuel DeWitt Proctor, who was a highly regarded African American pastor and professor. He wrote about a time one of his students, a young lady who was white, entered an elevator he was riding.

When the professor removed his hat, his student laughed. She said, "Dr. Proctor, why . . . did you take your hat off for me? You're living in the Victorian age."

Since the elevator was crowded, the professor asked her to step off on his floor for a moment, and he would explain. What he told her is something I believe many men and fathers need to hear:

> I'm not a Victorian, but some things stay in place from one generation to another, and certain manners stand for values I hold dear. I believe a society that ceases to respect women is on its way out. Women bear and raise our children . . . and they need our support and security through this process. When we forget that, the keystone of family and home is lost. . . . I believe that respect for women is the linchpin of the family and the society. Therefore, when you entered the elevator, I wanted you to have automatic, immediate, unqualified assurance that if the elevator caught fire, I would help you out through the top first. If a strange man boarded and began to slap you around . . . he would have to kill me first. If you fainted and slumped to the floor, I would stop everything and get you to a hospital. Now, it takes a lot of time to say all of that, so when I removed my hat, I meant all of the above.[2]

As Dr. Proctor looked at his student, her eyes were filled with tears. She was experiencing what far too many women in our society miss—a deep sense of worth and of being respected.

By removing his hat, Dr. Proctor was modeling honor. But his words made his modeling far more effective in that young woman's life.

In our efforts to *be* a sermon instead of just preaching one, let's not forget the power of words backed by actions.

Championship Checklist

The consistencies in our lives—good or bad—will leave a deep impression on our children. That's why we need to track our patterns and make adjustments when necessary. Measuring your patterns against the following statements can help.

1. *I am a good example to my children.* Try asking yourself, "What parts of my life would I never want my children to witness, and would be devastated if they acted the same way?" We can't excuse behavior in ourselves and condemn it in our children. When we object to out-of-control anger in them, for instance, we need to think about whether they're mirroring what they see in us.

2. *I try not to vary much in the way that I deal with my children.* Kids are students of consistency. Even at a young age, they can display uncanny accuracy in completing statements like, "When I do something wrong, Dad always . . ." or, "When something breaks, Mom always . . ." We may not think we're predictable, but our kids can identify our patterns. Our goal is to establish good ones.

3. *My children know what to expect of me.* This could be expanded to read, "My children know that I know what they expect of me, and I faithfully deliver." Kids are terrified by uncertainty as much as they are by chronic anger or harsh discipline. Our relationship with our kids isn't something to make up as we go along. If we're not intentional about our patterns, we're likely to fall back on habits that aren't positive or beneficial.

4. *I know what to do in a family crisis.* If your response is, "No, I don't," take a deep breath. Small and large family crises happen all the

time. You probably have a default pattern of reaction, even if you've never thought about it. Does that reaction help deal with the crisis or make it worse? If the family train is coming off the tracks, do you push it into the canyon?

Part of your role is to be a steadying, consistent presence that allows things to straighten out. If your past performance says you can do better, don't wait for the next crisis to have a family conversation about good things to do when life gets crazy. Letting family members know how you intend to change your approach will help them cooperate.

5. *I am predictable in the way I relate to my child.* For Championship Fathers, this means having a plan for loving, coaching, and modeling and carrying it out. Even in the ups and downs of raising a family, you'll never see a day in which you can say, "Today I don't have to do the fundamentals."

6. *I model behavior I want my children to have.* Effective fathering is all about telling *and* showing. It is never about, "Do as I say, not as I do." It takes courage and commitment to get to the place where you can honestly say, "Even though I'm not perfect, I'm generally living my life in a way I would be delighted to see my children live."

7. *I am usually levelheaded.* Are you able to keep your head when others around you are losing theirs? If this hasn't been your pattern, it's time to make a change. How do you handle the bathroom wars, the arguments, the festering sibling rivalry? What would be some better ways to respond? Show your family that you're learning to be a calming influence.

When I say it's hard to be consistent about pursuing consistency, I'm not kidding! But everyone in the house benefits from any progress you make in this area.

Walking the Talk

You'll never hear me boasting about my golfing skills, but not long ago I did have a golfing experience worth bragging about. I got to join some other men at Whistling Straits Golf Club in Wisconsin—a fabulous course.

And get this: I had a white caddy. No joke!

I was glad for his help, and didn't care what color he was. He knew that course and gave me some great tips along the way.

One morning, though, things got a little awkward. I'd arrived at the club and was putting my shoes on, getting ready to go out on the course. Just then a gentleman drove up and got out of a nice, big, sleek automobile. He came over to me.

"Would you get my bag for me?" he asked, assuming I was a club employee.

The people at the golf course were so embarrassed. They ran over and said, "No, no, no. This is Mr. Casey from the National Center for Fathering." They explained that I was playing golf there and what was going on, and it was no big deal.

A few minutes later, some of the guys in our group asked, "Carey, why didn't you put him in his place? Why didn't you get in his face? Why didn't you tell him who you are?"

I just smiled and said, "No, I dealt with that years ago."

As a child, I'd watched my father during the civil rights movement. We would be walking somewhere and he would be called the N-word. I remember how Dad would look at me as if to say, "Well, Son, evidently they don't know my name."

My daddy knew who he was, and he knew *whose* he was. He modeled dignity and self-control. I always liked the way Daddy "walked it" and not just "talked it."

We need to do both. We need to always be mindful about what our children are seeing in and through our lives. Through our modeling, we can choose what we pass on to them and to future generations—even in ways that could change the world.

ACTION POINTS

How to Model

Preschool

- Have you been promising your child that you would do something together? Make specific plans to follow through.
- Demonstrate self-control. Ask your children's mother how well you maintain your composure when tense or trying situations arise, and how you deal with anger.
- Take a hard look at your checkbook and your day planner. Do they reflect your true priorities?
- Have you scolded your child recently about a careless error he made? Go back and reassure him that though he makes mistakes sometimes, he is far more valuable to you than any things.
- What is the most important quality you can model for your children? Answer this question for yourself—and find a way to demonstrate that quality this week.
- Give your kids—even the younger ones—regular chores around the house. Be there to help them, and don't expect perfect results.

Elementary

- Show your children that a leader is also a servant. Find a meaningful way to serve each one.
- Ask family members if your habits reflect your true priorities. For example, does your cell phone interrupt family time?
- Make plans with another dad—and your kids—to help a single mom with a car repair, a household job, or some other task that she needs done.
- Look at your own media diet. Are there changes you need to make so you can be a better example for your children?

- Demonstrate your love for God by setting apart the Lord's Day as one for worship, rest, and family activities.
- Memorize a Bible passage you can repeat to yourself when you're losing your cool—such as James 1:19-20. Encourage your children to learn it, too.
- If possible, take your child to work for part of a day. Let him or her watch how you deal with issues that come up.
- Make sure your kids catch you reading often—especially the Bible.
- Whether or not you're married, be sure to express your convictions about marriage and fathering to your children. Then "walk the talk."
- Review the promises you've made to your child lately, and ask him or her how you're doing at following through.

Teen
- Volunteer with your teen at a hospital, soup kitchen, or nursing home, or reach out to someone in your neighborhood who has a specific need.
- Take your daughter on a "date" and talk about how she should expect to be treated by a boy who goes out with her.
- Treat your wife with respect, as you want your son to treat young ladies.
- Show your child your family budget. Talk about how your financial plans work month-to-month.
- As you drive with your teenager, think out loud about driving decisions you're making as you go.
- Practice saying the following words out loud, and be ready to use them with your children: "I was wrong. I'm sorry. Will you forgive me?"
- Talk with your wife about what you're modeling at home regarding health—what and where you eat, snacking, exercise, and regular checkups.

- Before a high-dollar purchase, talk with your teen about the factors you're considering. Ask for his or her thoughts on the matter.

For additional practical tips on fathering, subscribe to the National Center for Fathering's free e-mail, *fathers.com weekly,* at www.fathers.com/weekly. You'll also find articles on a wide range of fathering situations and challenges at www.fathers.com.

CHAPTER TEN

Modeling Faith
and Values

S o far, this book has been about creating a relationship and an environment that give you the best chance to pass to your children the core of who you are. Much of that core probably consists of your faith and values.

Why is it vital to transmit those things to your kids? Is it really possible? And how can you make sure that gift carries them to heights you can only dream of now—instead of weighing them down and even crushing them with spiritual-sounding rules?

That's where this chapter comes in.

Hands-on or Hands-off?

I've watched the growing popularity of a terrible, almost cowardly philosophy. It says something like, "Well, I wouldn't want to unduly influence my children with my beliefs. They ought to develop their own faith. So I won't try to tell them what I believe. I don't want to ram it down their throats. If they look closely, they'll pick up what I believe just by watching me. Otherwise, I want them to find their own way."

Said in the right tone of voice, those statements almost sound wise. But a parent who thinks that way is actually betraying his or her kids. It's like saying, "I'll teach my child how to tie his shoes and brush his teeth, but I won't teach him about God. That's too important. He can figure that out on his own."

The more important something is, the more we need to make sure our kids understand it. We don't teach them how to walk, then let them discover how to cross a busy highway on their own without any directions or warnings!

What can be more important than what we believe about right and wrong? If we've found the reality of God's love and grace in our lives, how can we not desire the same for our children?

Why would we teach our kids how to nourish their bodies and minds, but never get around to telling them how to nourish their souls? How could we talk to our children about the details of living in time and not tell them about the wonders of eternity?

We whisper "I love you" into their cribs, hoping the tone and familiarity of our voices will reassure and comfort them. Why wouldn't we add, "And what's more, God loves you, too!"?

Figuring Out Your Own Faith

I suspect that many parents who choose the "let my child discover faith on his own" approach are actually revealing that they don't have a faith worth passing on. What's true about love is true about faith: We can't give someone else what we don't have ourselves.

Not that many parents don't try. Young parents can be especially frantic about getting the "religious thing" right.

I observed as a pastor that one of the times a couple is most likely to show up at church is shortly after a baby is born. That sense of responsibility drives parents to do everything they can for their child, including trying to get some kind of protection from God by taking the child to church for baptism or dedication. They're looking for something from God even if they're not all that sure what He expects from them. Ceremonies in church usually call parents to make promises about "bringing up this child to know the Lord," but they may not have a clue about what that means.

Believe me, I understand how new parents feel about their job descriptions. I vividly remember looking through the window at the hospital and seeing the name "Casey" on one of those bassinets. Reality hit me in waves; I felt overwhelmed by the sudden responsibility. In fact, just looking at my newborn pushed responsibility buttons I didn't even know I had!

But I've also witnessed how a lot of parents interpret those responsibilities. They drop their kids off at church for Sunday school or other programs. They *send* their children to church.

I truly think a lot of those parents mean well. But I wonder if they ever pause to look at the experience from their children's point of view. The kids may be thinking, *Mom and Dad like to have a quiet, relaxed Sunday morning, so they send me off to church. I can't wait until I get old enough so I can have quiet, relaxed Sunday mornings.*

We can't tell our children, "This is important for you but it's not important for me," and expect them to believe us. If we demonstrate by our actions that involvement with people who are learning about God isn't important, they'll probably end up feeling the same way. If we want our kids to learn about God, they need to witness our interest and efforts in doing the same.

This is especially true when it comes to dads. A little-known study done in Switzerland[1] demonstrates that a father's involvement in modeling faith is critical.

The Swiss government tracked families, following church attendance by fathers and mothers as well as their children's attendance later in life. The study found that no matter how faithfully a mother attended church—regularly or occasionally—there was only a 2 percent chance of her children regularly attending church as adults *if the father had not attended as well.*

Amazingly, if the father went to church—regardless of how much Mom did—the likelihood of the child attending church as a grown-up increased to 60 to 75 percent!

Attending church doesn't make you a Christian, of course. But I think we can assume that if you aren't attending, you probably don't have a vibrant, ongoing faith to pass on to your children.

Fortunately, the heightened sense of responsibility that comes with parenthood can be a gift from God. For many dads and moms, it's a second chance to think about where their own lives are going.

I've run into a lot of people who didn't think much about going to heaven until they were holding a baby and wondering what was ultimately in store for that child. In fact, the attention-getting effect of babies may be behind some of Jesus' best-known words. In John 3:3, He basically told a grown man named Nicodemus, "Let Me shoot you straight, Nick. You're not going to get this relationship-with-God thing worked out until you are born again."

Nicodemus knew a lot, but he had trouble wrapping his mind around that concept. So Jesus schooled him: "For God so loved the world that he gave his one and only Son, that whoever believes in him shall not perish but have eternal life" (John 3:16).

People can make faith a strange and complicated thing, but Jesus made it simple and direct. Faith is about trusting—believing in—Him.

Even if faith has always been mysterious, confusing, and complicated for you, here's a chance to boil it down. Faith in Jesus is about trusting Him with your future—even your eternal future.

A missionary once said, "If you find someone more trustworthy than Jesus, then you will probably trust that person. But I have never found or heard of someone more trustworthy than Jesus, so I'm trusting Him."

The real problem most people have with faith isn't that they've found someone more trustworthy than Jesus. It's that they haven't really looked at Him as someone uniquely capable of being trusted with their past, present, and future! Often this reveals our deeper issue of not wanting to turn over control of our lives, even to God.

I'm not trying to ram a point of view down your throat or urge you to ram it down your children's throats. But I'd be doing you a great disservice if I didn't shoot you straight about the crucial truth that you've got to have a faith in order to pass it on to your kids.

If you're thinking right now, *I've got to find a faith,* then I want to point you to Jesus Christ. If you give Him a chance, I'm certain you'll find Him trustworthy in every way.

Impressing Your Kids

Earlier in this book I mentioned Deuteronomy 6:7-9, a powerful Bible passage reminding parents of their responsibility to transmit God's commands to their children:

> Impress them on your children. Talk about them when you sit at
> home and when you walk along the road, when you lie down and
> when you get up. Tie them as symbols on your hands and bind them
> on your foreheads. Write them on the doorframes of your houses and
> on your gates.

God's commands are to be on our hearts, and we're to *impress* them on our children. What does that word conjure up in your mind?

Here's one thing it *doesn't* mean: a monotonous time of lecturing your kids or reading more Bible verses than they can possibly absorb. If God's instructions are really on your heart, then you need to express personally and persuasively to your children your hopes and dreams for them to follow Christ.

When I think of impressing God's commands on our children, I always think of my own father. He had this one down. When he took us on all those car rides, he didn't preach to us about sex or drugs or anything else. But he did let us know what was on his heart.

That mattered to us because he'd built a *relationship* with us. He'd earned the right to be heard. We knew that if we did the wrong thing, we would break his heart in addition to sinning against God. I think many kids today don't have that sense of accountability to their earthly father.

My dad let us know how important God's commands were to him without creating an atmosphere of fear and danger. He impressed truth on us by building a strong relationship and showing us how he felt. If it mattered to him, it mattered to us.

Dad was practicing Deuteronomy 6:7 when he did that. The verse urges parents to talk about God's Word "when you walk along the road." We were just experiencing the modern equivalent as we cruised in our automobile.

Pop showed us how God's truth touched every facet of life. He didn't have a Sunday life distinct from the rest of the week. It was all one. There was no escape from his quiet consistency—and the indelible impression he left on us.

Consider the Source

Pop not only shared his values; he let us know where they came from.

On a hot afternoon in August 1963, he'd stood with thousands gathered on the mall in Washington, D.C. He'd listened to an eloquent man speak, a man whose words rang from the steps just below Abraham Lincoln's marble feet, echoing between the monuments, sinking into the hearts of those gathered.

Change was in the air. Hope had drawn men and women like my father to that place. Folks just knew something was up; it felt like history was being made!

That day set the bar of possibilities high for the multiethnic crowd. The difficulties and pain of the years that followed might have overwhelmed many if they hadn't had those phrases still ringing in their minds.

Fortunately, the words of the Reverend Martin Luther King, Jr. were recorded so that generations yet unborn would have a chance to experience his deeply moving message. They became etched on the soul of a nation. My own children, born decades after that day, have listened to the measured cadence and hard-edged wisdom of those words:

I have a dream . . .
I have a dream . . .
I have a dream . . .

> I have a dream that my four little children will one day live in a nation where they will be judged not by the color of their skin but by the content of their character.

At the center of those remarks is a man speaking passionately as a father, expressing his deepest longings about his children. Dr. King was more than an African American prophet confronting a nation about the need for racial reconciliation. He was ultimately a father thundering to other fathers about their deep responsibility to parent their children.

He was trying to raise four kids, just as I am. Also like me, he didn't want his children to be judged by external factors but by character—by the kind of faith that makes a person's whole life "work."

My dad was there that day. I know that when Dr. King talked about his children, my father thought about me, my sister, and my brother.

My father passed Dr. King's dream to me, too. He deepened it and broadened it. As part of that process, Dad took me aside like an ancient patriarch and gave me a blessing that has directed my life ever since.

It happened the day I told him, "I wish I could have been a grown-up back in 1963, when all that was happening with civil rights."

"No, Son," he replied. "You're going to be part of something even greater than that." I believe he was setting me free to be part of something even more profound than the reconciliation of the races in my country.

Dr. King longed for a day when race wouldn't matter, but character would be the focus. Once we stop judging by race, character can take the stage. But who and what will determine the content of a child's character? Who's in charge of character development?

We fathers—and mothers—bear that responsibility. Others can help, but we're crucial.

The Reverend Martin Luther King, Jr. was a coach. Many of his sermons read like classic locker room talks, given to a nation. What Vince Lombardi was to football, Dr. King was to the civil rights movement and to a nation coming to terms with basic dignity for people.

As an adult child of the civil rights movement, I'm deeply grateful to those who pushed America closer to being a nation where all people are treated equally, as God created them to be. I'm also grateful to my father— who was clear about his faith and values, who let me know the *why* behind them, and was intentional about passing them on through word and deed.

The Purpose-Driven Pop

As contented and fulfilled as my dad was, he wanted his kids to go beyond where he'd been. By effectively modeling his faith and values, he gave us the tools we needed.

More than once I've responded to situations in a way that caused Melanie or someone else to ask, "Carey, what made you say that?" or, "How did you know what to do there?"

At first I wasn't sure where I got the idea. But then I remembered: I watched Pop handle a situation like that once! I just did what he did.

There also have been times when I've run into a question or issue that stumps me. But then I ask, "What would Pop say or do in this situation?" Often an event from my childhood, something I haven't thought about for years, will appear in my mind as an answer.

The most important things in life, like faith, Pop didn't delegate to other people. True, we went to church with him and talked about the sermons we heard. But he wanted direct input when it came to spiritual matters. And he got it—because the way he modeled the Christian faith couldn't be separated from the package that was his life.

So much of dad's daily life was intentional. He wasn't just going through the motions; he had a plan. We've heard a lot recently about the "purpose-driven life," and that was Pop.

Because I'm convinced he had a reason for almost everything he did, I like to revisit the events of my childhood. My experiences as a father have allowed me to understand why he chose certain pathways. My brother, sister, and I were always on his mind, influencing his decisions.

For example, my folks never *sent* me to Sunday school. We went *together*. In church I sat next to Pop—a learning experience all by itself. I can still feel the vibrations that seemed to come from him, through the pew and into my body, as he hummed or verbalized his agreement with what he was hearing. I paid attention during sermons because I wanted to know what made him say softly, "Oh, yes," or, "That's true!" or even, "You can say that again, Brother!"

My father's responsiveness to truth had a deep effect on me. Sometimes today I have to remember that in a lot of churches I get to visit, folks are used to sitting real quiet. I know this is supposed to help them pay attention, but sometimes I think it just helps people stay asleep, if you know what I mean.

When people talk about participating in worship, I think Pop had—and I have—a good idea of what's involved. Sitting right next to Dad put me in touch with his soul.

Do your kids know what moves you? Do they understand what touches the core of who you are? Do they know your favorite hymn or chorus, even if they call it an "oldie"? Do they see you reading the Bible? Can they recite your favorite verse, if you have one?

Transmitting values and faith isn't just about what kids *happen* to see and hear when they watch you. The process often needs to be deliberate on your part, especially if you haven't been aware of how important it is and need to catch up.

Repetition of your patterns is vital, too. One time won't do it. The most important things they need to hear and see over and over again. They may even complain, "Not *that* again, Dad!" But that's when you know they'll never forget it!

A Purposeful Plan

One father discovered the value of planning a few years ago when his three young children were open to a lesson in faith and values.

A terrible famine in Ethiopia was getting a lot of news coverage on TV, and appeals for help were coming in the mail. Pictures of suffering children often appeared on the screen and in print. After one news story aired, the seven-year-old approached Dad and asked, "Can't we send some money to help those kids?"

Dad said, "Well, let me think about that a little."

I realize that's a trick we parents use sometimes to *avoid* thinking about something, but this father wanted to use this opportunity to teach his children a deeper lesson. He took the time to come up with a plan.

Finally he gathered the family and announced, "I think it would be a great idea if we sent some money to help those kids in Ethiopia. Who's got some money?"

One child was still a toddler, but the two older boys looked at each other for a moment. Then the older one said, "You've got the money, Dad."

Dad said, "Well, it's really our family's money—and if we give some of it to those Ethiopian kids, we won't have it for us. So do you still want to do this?"

Both boys nodded their heads eagerly.

Then their father described a project. "All right. Since you want to do this, let's give those kids the money that we would normally spend for food for ourselves this next weekend. We will choose to go hungry for two days so that we can help those kids who are hungry all the time. Are you guys with me?"

These were smart kids. Before agreeing, they wanted more information. "So, we can't eat anything for two days?" they asked, sounding worried.

Dad said, "We'll have a nice supper on Friday night. Then we won't have any meals all day Saturday. Then on Sunday, we won't eat breakfast or lunch, but we'll have a supper to end our fast. You can drink lots of water during that time, but we won't eat any food." He knew he had healthy kids who wouldn't be harmed by skipping a few meals.

The boys agreed, but the younger one still looked worried. His father asked, "What are you thinking, Son?"

The boy pointed to one of the hunger relief brochures and said, "After I don't eat for two days, will I look like one of those kids?"

That's when Dad knew that the reality of what they were doing was sinking in. He assured his boy that he would be fine.

It turned out to be a memorable weekend. The most meaningful moment came when the family discussed why a loving God would allow suffering in the world.

Those kids, now grown with children of their own, have never forgotten that experience. It was a weekend of concentrated transmission of faith and values.

Transmitting Without Controlling

When you're concerned about passing along faith and values, it's tempting to take a shortcut: trying to *control* your kids' thinking and behavior instead of *influencing* it. Besides ignoring the fact that God gave our kids free will, that approach doesn't work.

I faced this issue when both my daughters wanted to get married. That led to a lot of reflecting on how I'd invested in them and what kind of young ladies they'd become. It was difficult to let go, but I learned much in the process.

Christie and Patrice both came to a point when their relationships were getting pretty serious. They both wanted to know, "Dad, do you think this is *the one*?" They weren't just making conversation; they really wanted to know what their old dad thought.

I'm thankful that I could sincerely give my blessing on both occasions. I don't think either of them was worried about what I would say, but I could tell that my words—my blessing—brought them a little extra comfort and confidence. They really loved these guys, and I supported their decisions all the way. Both girls ended up getting married during the same year.

Thinking back on those two conversations, I believe God helped me see the true value of the relationship between fathers and daughters. And I saw the true character of my daughters revealed.

Choosing a marriage partner was a huge decision for them. But I knew it had to be *up to them* to make wise choices. I couldn't try to control that part of their lives.

Believe me, there had been times when I wished I could have controlled them. Several of the guys they'd brought home, Melanie and I could tell, would not have been good for them. We shared those observations with our daughters, but never tried to control them. It was always their decision.

Modeling isn't controlling. In most cases, control will just embitter your son or daughter and drive him or her away.

You have to hold your tongue sometimes. You have to let your kids go in small and big ways. You have to trust in the investment you've made in them through the years, and trust that God will continue to guide and protect them.

Championship Checklist

Here's one more research-based checklist. I hope these measuring tools have been helpful to you.

Personally, I've found these useful in my own pursuit of Championship Fathering. I always seem to note an area in which I'm slipping or one in which I need to respond to a particular challenge. These lists keep a game plan before me; they hold me accountable for making progress.

How well do these statements apply to you?

1. *I model behavior that I want my children to have.* I've repeated this one from the last chapter's list because it underscores the importance of modeling a life of faith before our children. We want to speak about and behave toward God in a way we'd like our children to emulate. That requires listening, watching, talking about our faith, and living it out. We can't delegate these functions to others.

2. *I read Scripture with my children often.* Reading the Bible can be a great conversation stimulator for kids. But their questions probably will drive you

to do some studying on your own. That's good! We and our kids also need to get beyond admiring the Bible for what it is (God's Word) and get serious about what it says (also God's Word).

3. *I pray with my children.* There's nothing like praying with your kids to help you develop the habit of praying on your own. Just as you want your kids to talk—I mean *really talk*—with you, our heavenly Father desires interaction with you and your kids. And remember, simple is better when it comes to prayer.

4. *We have a family worship time in our home.* The challenge here is finding ways to acknowledge God as a family. It can be an extension of praying together at bedtime or mealtimes, or taking time on Sunday evening to talk as a family about what you experienced in church earlier that day. Doing this consistently won't be easy; you'll have to work at it. As a dad, you really need to start this race, set the pace, and keep things going.

5. *I talk about spiritual things with my children.* The topic of faith doesn't have to be relegated to certain times and places. It affects every decision we make, every moment we live. Deuteronomy 6:7 implies that opportunities to impress an awareness of God on our kids will come up throughout the day. If you're not sure where to start, check out Deuteronomy 5–6 and talk through the Ten Commandments (Exodus 20) with your kids.

6. *I stress the importance of spiritual values to my children.* Doing this verbally is important, but we drive home the true importance of spiritual values in our lives by the way we actually live. This may involve giving our children permission to "call" us on our inconsistencies. For instance, if we make a big deal over how Jesus told us not to worry and our children witness how we fret over little things, they're right to point out that we're talking the talk but not walking the walk.

7. *I am a good example to my children.* This one is also repeated from the last chapter, with faith and values in mind. The real test of this statement comes when we become grandparents. If your children parent the way you parented them, will you feel good about that? Will they have to pick up faith

and values from someone else? The way you and I father will affect our children, grandchildren, great-grandchildren, and beyond. We can't take lightly the invitation to step up to the pursuit of Championship Fathering.

Who's Got the Time?

In today's world, many dads work long hours. Kids' schedules are jam-packed. There's no obvious time for extended or regular family reading of God's Word and spiritual conversations. Where are we supposed to find time for modeling faith and values?

We can't use that as an excuse. We need to get creative and see our lives as a spiritual training ground. We need to invest real time, but can do that by grabbing bits and pieces of life here and there.

In a given week, maybe you'll spend an hour as a family in prayer, reading the Bible, or having a short devotion. Add a few minutes of one-on-one time with each child every week, and you're well on your way.

Make the most of the time you're already with your children. That will go a long way toward helping them understand how God's truth is relevant to their daily lives.

For example, time spent driving kids around can be useful. Talk about things happening in your life and theirs; ask how they've seen God at work, or about friends who might need God's love.

As you do all this, don't expect perfection. Keep cool if you're interrupted, or if funny things happen.

That's what Joe and his wife have to do. They often read from the Book of Proverbs with their two sons, sometimes while they're riding to school in the car. One day, Joe's second-grade son was reading in Proverbs 5. Things were going great until he got to verses 18 and 19:

> May your fountain be blessed,
>   and may you rejoice in the wife of your youth.
> A loving doe, a graceful deer—

may her *beasts* satisfy you always,
may you ever be captivated by her love. (italics added)

Now, that word isn't really "beasts." The boy missed an "R" in there somewhere. But Joe and his wife didn't think that was the best time to correct him and answer all the questions that would surely follow. For the moment, they had to just suppress their laughter and keep going.

Despite occasional glitches like that, Proverbs is a great book for families to read together. You can read for several minutes or just a verse or two; every page is filled with nuggets to ponder and discuss with your children. Read them with your kids, Dad. You might want to read ahead a little, though, so you're ready for what your children may find!

Mealtime is critical for families, too. Work at having meals together as often as possible. Think about the content of your conversation around the table. Try bringing up a question to discuss—perhaps a challenge your kids are likely to face. Ask, "How would you handle that?" Then direct the discussion toward the wisdom found in God's Word.

Taking children along for routine errands also provides modeling moments. Your kids get a chance to see you out in the world, making decisions, being responsible, living out your faith. You may not be aware of it, but transmission of faith and values is happening along the way.

We have such limited time with our kids. But God will bring teachable moments our way. Look for those openings and use them to point to God's glory and His plan for the lives of your children.

Be a Model Storyteller

I believe at least part of one of the psalms in the Old Testament was written for dads:

O my people, hear my teaching;
listen to the words of my mouth.

I will open my mouth in parables,
I will utter hidden things, things from of old—
what we have heard and known,
what our fathers have told us.
We will not hide them from their children;
we will tell the next generation
the praiseworthy deeds of the LORD,
his power, and the wonders he has done.
He decreed statutes for Jacob
and established the law in Israel,
which he commanded our forefathers
to teach their children,
so the next generation would know them,
even the children yet to be born,
and they in turn would tell their children.
Then they would put their trust in God
and would not forget his deeds
but would keep his commands. (Psalm 78:1-7)

What a picture of how to pass a living faith on to our children! Among the stories we tell our children, God's stories should feature prominently.

We should open our mouths in parables—stories that communicate a powerful lesson. We should tell our children "things from of old"—what our fathers may have told us. We mustn't hide the great lessons from them.

I know you're not hiding these lessons intentionally. But if you're a follower of Jesus, are you telling the next generation about the Lord's "praiseworthy deeds" and "wonders"? What stories can you tell about God's intervention in your life? Prayers that were answered? Moments of unexpected provision? Small miracles that opened your eyes to His love? Experiences that demonstrated His majesty and power?

Have you told your children and grandchildren? Do you see God working in your church, your small group, your neighborhood? Point those things out to your kids! Let them experience God's power through you.

And then, as Psalm 78 says, give them a vision for their own future—how someday *they* will tell these or similar stories to their own children, passing on that legacy of faith.

Your Toughest Modeling Job

What's your number-one fathering assignment? Our research indicates that a wide array of objectives make up Championship Fathering, but I'm convinced that one goal belongs near the top. It's something we tend to forget: modeling for our children what God is like as a heavenly Father.

In a sense, showing my children what God is like is impossible. He's perfect; I'm an average dad. The difference between God and me approaches infinity. Still, many of our children's ideas about God will be based on their relationships with us. I don't think we can be reminded too often.

If children grow up with an earthly father who's absent or emotionally distant, it will be much more difficult for them to view God as a present, actively involved heavenly Father. If a dad is inconsistent, overly harsh, or rigid—as I am sometimes—his children will likely relate to God based on those experiences. Fathering creates impressions about God for our children, and it's up to us to make the most of our opportunity.

How can we show our kids what God is like? Consider just a few of His attributes: He's loving, just, merciful, slow to anger, available. He protects and provides. Does that sound like the kind of father you want to be? No doubt that's the kind your kids need.

You're never going to be all-powerful, all-knowing, or always present. But that's how your kids will look at you—especially when they're very young.

Make every effort to reflect the character of God in your life. That means you probably should get to know Him as well as possible yourself! Then you'll be able to give your children a pretty good taste of what kind of Father He is.

What Will They Remember?

My friend Bryan Davis from All-Pro Dads asked an interesting question recently: Do you know the names of your great-grandfathers? Or your great-grandmothers?

Maybe you do, but I suspect most of us don't. Nor do many of us know what they did with their lives, what they stood for, what they believed in.

In the grand scheme of things, knowing ancestors' names may not seem like such a big deal. But think of it this way: Will your great-grandchildren know *your* name?

If present trends continue, probably not. So you and I may be three or four generations from being forgotten—historically extinct!

I don't know about you, but I want to leave a better, more lasting legacy than that. I don't mean that I want my descendants to remember how great I was or how much I accomplished, that I ran for senator or built a world-famous business. No, I want to be remembered as just one of many in a long line who built a reputation of high character, a close-knit family, and a deep faith in Christ. That's what it's all about!

Our children will be grown up sooner than we realize. It staggers me to think of Chance as an adult with children of his own—but it seemed to happen in a heartbeat with his older brother and sisters. I want to equip Chance for that future, and modeling is an indispensable part of the process.

That's how we can stand the test of time as dads—by ensuring that loving, coaching, and modeling are the pattern of our lives. We can be the connected, involved fathers our children need us to be—one day at a time.

Staying on track requires staying close to God. Make your relationship with God a daily exercise. Introducing your kids to your faith and values depends in part on how much you trust your heavenly Father and how familiar you've gotten with Him over the years.

You've been transmitting your real faith and real values to your children, whether you wanted to or not, from the moment they were born. The earlier you start being intentional about the process, the better!

The payoffs won't always be immediate. Sometimes you have to wait for years to see the results. But hang in there. Involvement in Championship Fathering has its trophies—moments in which our kids make the right choices. That's when we realize in a whole new way how worthwhile it is to invest ourselves in our children's lives.

Championship Fathering challenges us to ask, "What can I do today to invest in my children and build a lasting, godly legacy?" Are there activities you've been meaning to do with them? Talks you've wanted to have?

It's time to make those things a priority. Why put off until sometime or never what you can start doing today?

 ACTION POINTS

Modeling Faith and Values

Preschool

- In your spiritual training plan for your children, include time to just have fun together and create a closer relationship.
- Try occasionally writing out your prayers for your child. Save them and give them all to him or her during a significant time in his or her life.
- Be faithful in a regular "quiet time" with God. It will influence your children when they see that you place high value on it, especially if they notice positive results in your life.
- Read a Bible storybook with your child on your lap.

- Take a walk or have a picnic with your child, pointing out colors, textures, sounds, and smells you encounter in nature. Be sure to give credit to God for His handiwork.
- If your church has a food pantry to aid the needy, or a food drive is scheduled in your area, let your child help you pick out canned and boxed goods at the grocery store and bring them to the collection point.

Elementary

- Using an example from one of your child's interests—sports, science, animals, the arts—teach him or her a simple truth about God's character or a biblical virtue. For ideas, try the book *Faith-Launch* by John Trent and Jane Vogel (Focus on the Family/ Tyndale, 2008).
- After church, with your children present, ask your wife what she learned there. Then ask your children what they learned.
- Find a story in the Bible where Jesus demonstrates humility (such as washing the disciples' feet in John 13) and read it with your children. See how many ways they can think of to serve others.
- During the Olympics or after watching another sports event, look for scriptures with an athletic theme (1 Corinthians 9:24-27; Hebrews 12:1-3; 2 Timothy 2:5) and read them with your child. Ask, "How could this apply to you and me?"
- What will heaven be like? Ask your children what they think, and then find answers together in Scripture.
- Share with your kids one recent success and one current challenge in your life. Ask your children to pray for you.
- Read together from the Book of Proverbs, keeping a list of your favorite sayings.
- Ask your wife for ideas on how you can serve her; then get your children involved in helping you carry them out.

- Memorize Bible verses with your kids and quote them to each other regularly.
- Schedule time at least once or twice a week to read the Bible and pray with each of your children—even if it's only for five minutes.

Teen

- Ask your child which kids at school need prayer, and pray for them as a family. Pray for your child's relationship with these kids, too.
- During TV commercials, ask your kids thought-provoking questions like, "What's the message behind this?" "How do they want us to respond?" "How would our lives really be different if we did what they're suggesting?"
- Encourage your kids to spend at least 5 or 10 minutes each day in Bible study and prayer—and make sure they see you doing the same thing.
- Give your children real-life chances to see your faith in action—and to express their own faith. Volunteer together to help those in need—on a missions trip, in a homeless shelter, or when car problems strand motorists along the side of the road.
- If your family tree contains one or more ancestors who modeled a strong faith, tell your teen about that person; share stories and photos if possible.
- Help your teen find at least one adult in your church who can give him or her good advice on how to reach a career goal.
- Search the Bible with your teen for several verses that apply to struggles he or she is going through.

For additional practical tips on fathering, subscribe to the National Center for Fathering's free e-mail, *fathers.com weekly,* at www.fathers.com/weekly. You'll also find articles on a wide range of fathering situations and challenges at www.fathers.com.

CHAPTER ELEVEN

A Vision for the World

S everal years ago, our family moved from the suburbs to the inner city. I was convinced that God wanted me to enter relationships with those around me—not just as a weekend project or a mission trip, but as a way of life. So I accepted an invitation to become a co-pastor of a church in Chicago. We moved into a different world.

In that neighborhood there were drug dealers on street corners. When I walked outside my house, everyone asked me for money. Conflicts often were resolved with guns, not words.

Little kids would ask my wife, "What is that thing on your finger?"

And she'd say, "That's my wedding ring. Mr. Casey is my husband."

For those kids, seeing a married couple was a rare thing. They didn't know what a healthy, intact family was like.

Through the Lawndale Community Church, we were able to make a difference. The church bought some of the biggest drug houses and tore them down. We built a gymnasium, a medical clinic, and a system through which people could receive help while learning to work and maintain their dignity.

I'm telling you this because we need a similar approach to another problem.

I'm talking about father-absence. It's a cancer spreading in our culture, a serious condition that requires major surgery, not just a Band-Aid.

And it isn't only a metaphor. It's a real threat that's getting worse. If things don't change, our children and grandchildren will live in a completely different society.

We fathers must be the catalyst to alter our culture's course. We have to go outside our comfort zones to bring parents and kids positive values, really care for them, and help them find new lives and hope.

Championship Fathering starts with you and me in our own homes. But it can't stop there. And it won't—when we really get involved in our children's lives, doing the fathering fundamentals.

The Fathering Deficit

I hope this book has introduced you to some ideas that will help you reach your goals as a father. But I have to tell you that, in the world we're living in today, being a great dad to your own kids is just not enough.

The United States, where I live, leads the world in fatherless homes. Almost half of the school-age children in America live in a home without their father present. The fathering deficit experienced by these children causes them to face a whole host of challenges.

But the impact of this deficit extends far beyond these children. It affects our culture as a whole. If you think we're facing trouble today with poverty and crime, just wait to see what the future will look like for your children and grandchildren if we don't reverse the current trends.

I believe this is the most ignored major crisis in our culture. So at the National Center for Fathering we've been asking ourselves a question: What will it take to reverse the fathering deficit?

Our response is to start by recognizing the seriousness of the problem and taking responsibility for our part in reversing the trends. Then we cast a vision for a changed culture that understands and encourages Championship Fathering.

We believe that men who take their fathering responsibilities seriously are best equipped to turn the tide and erase the fathering deficit. And I believe that you—and committed dads like you—are the key to creating that culture of Championship Fathering.

Are you with me?

Facing the Problem

How serious is the fathering deficit? Here's a little experiment I conduct on a regular basis.

When I hear about any societal crisis, disaster, or problem, I ask, "How would responsible fathering have made a difference in this situation?" I usually find a "father angle" right away. In many news stories about children acting in violent or self-destructive ways, for example, the father is not only absent from the child's life—he's absent from the story.

In December 2007, the fourth U.S. mall shooting rampage of the year occurred in Omaha, Nebraska. A quick read of news stories about that incident and the others reveals one glaring point of similarity: fathers were absent from these young men's lives. In the reporting, friends and mothers are frequently quoted—but not a word from Dad. Father doesn't get mentioned and he doesn't get blamed.

In other words, we aren't even *expecting* fathers to be responsible anymore, so we don't include them in our analysis. The fathering vacuum just isn't addressed. And when it is, the messenger is often attacked for speaking the truth.

I've been amazed at the responses Bill Cosby has received for using his position as a voice among African Americans to speak boldly about the need for the black community to stop playing the "blame game"—to take more responsibility for problems like out-of-wedlock pregnancies, fatherlessness, gang proliferation, and the general tendency to fix responsibility on outsiders or society at large. He's refreshingly blunt: Blame doesn't fix things. As a result, he's been attacked for daring to see beyond blaming.

Cosby is pointing to a way of personal responsibility that challenges all of us, no matter what our racial or social background may be. The mirror he holds up to everyone shows the effects of irresponsible parenting.

Fixing the Problem

Acknowledging the fathering deficit isn't an objective. It's a door we need to pass through on our way to practical solutions.

The things that would change society most deeply don't cost a lot of money. But they do take hours and effort. Fathers make a difference by investing their time and energy in their children, determining to be there for them.

We also need to admit that fathers don't duplicate a mother's role; both parents' parts in a child's life are complementary. Having two parents doesn't mean you have an extra one you can easily get along without. Mom and Dad are not interchangeable.

It takes two to make a baby—and to raise one. Single parents face the necessity of raising children alone, but that's clearly not the original design. Our society has come close to calling single parenting an ideal, but few who've tried it actually agree.

Not long ago I was in Washington, D.C., meeting about a project designed to help fathers and families. I saw stately, historic buildings—and some of the toughest, most desperate neighborhoods. What really stayed with me were some of the faces I saw as I drove and walked the streets. Numerous men stood on corners, just hanging out, with dark stares in their eyes. They looked utterly hopeless.

Remembering those faces reminds me of some verses from the New Testament. Jesus was going through towns and villages, healing people and sharing the good news about hope in God. After watching Jesus, Matthew wrote this:

> When he saw the crowds, he had compassion on them, because they were harrassed and helpless, like sheep without a shepherd. Then he said to his disciples, "The harvest is plentiful but the workers are few.

Ask the Lord of the harvest, therefore, to send out workers into his harvest field." (Matthew 9:36-38)

When it comes to erasing the fathering deficit, we need to look at the world around us with the eyes of Jesus. We start with our own houses, but we can't stop there—not just because we have a responsibility to help others, but because we need their help, too!

In some places the problem is out in the open—inner city areas, divorce courts, gang turf wars, classrooms in chaos. In most places, the problem is hidden until parents and children begin to share their heartache. If we let the fathering deficit continue to grow, we'll harvest an ever-expanding crop of sadness, bitterness, purposelessness, and violence.

Helping fathers is one of the best answers to many of society's ills. Turn a dad's life around, making him a responsible and loving leader of his family, and he'll make a difference for his children and others.

Can you raise your sights beyond fathering your own children? Can you encourage another child in your sphere of influence—extended family, church, your child's school or sports team? Can you enlist other dads to join you in a commitment to Championship Fathering?

The Power of One

You may wonder whether your efforts would really make a difference. After all, being an effective father to your own kids is hard enough. How can one dad change a neighborhood, much less a nation?

When I feel that way, it helps to think about George Washington Carver.

I consider him to be one of the influential models in my life, even though he died several years before I was born. He made innovative advances in science and agriculture, and was a cultural revolutionary as well. He was a shining example of someone who worked hard and lived a humble, simple life.

The school I attended as a boy in Salem, Virginia, was named after him. At its 1940 dedication, illness prevented Mr. Carver from attending. But he sent a telegram that read, "I trust that every pupil will regard the splendid school building as an opportunity to make their lives count 100 percent as American citizens." That statement became part of the school's heritage.

That simple encouragement to make my life count 100 percent inspired me as a boy, and it continues to do so today. When I returned to that school a few years ago and spoke to the students as part of Black History Month, I read Dr. Carver's telegram to them. When he sent it, the school was all African American, but now is integrated. His message to all students who would attend there applies to black, white, brown, red, or yellow—everyone. One man's words and example live on to inspire generations.

You may be just one man, but some of the things you say and do will ring in your children's memories for a long time—maybe even in the memories of their friends and their friends' families. Look for opportunities to speak and act in ways that inspire them to do great things.

The Power of a Team

If one person can make a difference, teaming up with others can make even more.

I'm not sure the 2007-2008 Green Bay Packers had much of a vision for their season beyond doing better than the year before. The youngest team in the NFL, led by the "ancient" Brett Favre, had ended the previous season strong, but had a long way to go to be considered elite again. Much to everyone's surprise, including their own, they went 13 wins, 3 losses for the regular season.

Young players played like veterans. Old Brett Favre played like a kid with a wise man's self-control. Their record earned them a playoff game, a bye week to recuperate, and sudden dreams of a championship season.

Their playoff home game was scheduled against the Seattle Seahawks. It was a beautiful Wisconsin winter day with snow-laden clouds hovering over the cheering crowd.

Green Bay received the opening kickoff and set up deep in their end for the first play, a high percentage throw out to the halfback drifting to the right flat. Most hearts in Lambeau Stadium skipped a beat when Ryan Grant bobbled the pass, fell, got up, and then fumbled the ball when he was hit. The pigskin was recovered by Seattle, which immediately converted on the next play. Only seconds had elapsed on the game clock, but Green Bay was down seven points.

With kickoff number two, the Packers' offense came back on the field. One play later, the same young halfback fumbled when he hit the line of scrimmage. Seahawks recovered. Seattle scored again.

It was the Packers' worst nightmare coming true in living color. The snow began to fall. Barely a minute into the game, the Packers were in a 14-point hole.

Fortunately, there were still 58 minutes to play. And what a game it was! Green Bay eventually won 42 to 20.

The Packers played as a team. They got down early, but didn't stay down. They didn't lose their composure or try to get everything back immediately. Together, they patiently persevered to victory.

In our battle with the fathering deficit, we're definitely down more than 14 points. What's it going to take to win?

It's going to take a team of committed dads like you—dads who will love, coach, and be models for their kids, dads who will encourage other children, dads who will enlist other fathers to join the team.

It will have to be a *big* team if we're going to erase the fathering deficit. At the National Center for Fathering, we envision it this way: You and I are joined by just 10 percent of the other dads, the ones we hope will make the Championship Fathering commitment.

It doesn't sound like many, just 1 in 10. But it would be a powerful force. Standing shoulder-to-shoulder, we'd create a line that stretches from Boston to San Diego. More importantly, the children of those 6.5 million dads and the other kids encouraged by them would benefit.

Remember, you're not alone. Your teammates are here for you.

The outcome isn't certain, and it's going to take a lot of time to develop and practice responsible fathering. Good results may not happen immediately, either. But being part of the Championship Fathering team is all about long-term determination. After all, we aren't just dads on Father's Day; we're dads every day.

JOIN THE CHAMPIONSHIP FATHERING TEAM!

Visit www.fathers.com/cf and make your commitment today. The National Center for Fathering will provide weekly encouragement by e-mail as you seek to fulfill this commitment to Championship Fathering:

1. I will *love* my children.
2. I will *coach* my children.
3. I will *model* for my children.
4. I will *encourage* other children.
5. I will *enlist* other dads to join the Championship Fathering team.

A Lasting Legacy

Pop used to take our family to the carnival when it came to town. There were candy apples and animals, and the dunk tank was always a big hit.

It seemed my dad could do anything. At the "test your strength" game, I watched him bring that big hammer down with amazing force and ring the bell. Everyone applauded, and I was really shocked—and proud. He was so vibrant and strong back then.

Later, on the very same piece of land where the carnival had been, a new wing of the Veterans Administration hospital was built.

Still later, when my dad had Parkinson's and was declining, he lived in the care center there. I would take my family down to see him.

Because he had worked at the hospital for 30 years, Dad knew everybody there. There were doctors and nurses who spoke to him with admiration and respect. We met many other patients, some injured in Vietnam, Korea, or World War II, some with limited mental capacities. My dad treated all those guys with great dignity.

He would introduce us to them and say, "Carey, this is Mr. So-and-so." I can't remember Dad ever defining these men in terms of their challenges. He didn't demean them at all.

As the Parkinson's progressed, Dad's legs stopped functioning. Eventually we knew the end was getting close.

On one of our last visits, we all helped him out of bed and into his wheelchair. We wheeled him down to another room for physical therapy. There we all hugged, kissed, and parted.

After we dropped him off, we walked back to the car. But this time we just kind of stood there.

I thought about those days at the carnival, right there on the same ground. I thought about how he had been so strong and energetic.

The emotions flooded over me. So did the tears.

The rest of my family began to cry, too. We all had memories of Pop.

We knew that aging and sickness are part of life. But my older kids could remember their grandfather picking them up, chasing them around the yard, and so much more.

It was hard, but it was also a precious time. In our sadness, we were honoring my dad for what he meant to us.

What I'm about to tell you might sound a little strange. But I want to encourage you to live in such a way that your kids feel great about crying when you're gone.

I've found this to be true: People who have been loved well, been coached well, and had a consistent model are people who express their appreciation partly through tears.

I'm convinced that if you remember and practice these three fathering fundamentals—loving, coaching, and modeling—you'll experience winning seasons in your life as a father and leave a lasting legacy for your children and grandchildren.

Look for other dads who have a passion for Championship Fathering; create a team of mutual encouragers.

And keep the line open between you and your heavenly Father, the ultimate Lover, Coach, and Model for both you and your children.

Epilogue

I now consider myself a father of seven. That's because my three oldest children have spouses, and those in-laws are definitely not outlaws, if you know what I mean. They're family, just like my two daughters and two sons.

My oldest daughter, Christie, married Shunton, a high school principal. I met him at our church and began mentoring him; later he met my daughter in our home. I'm glad things worked out from there the way they did.

Shunton came from a tough background—very poor, and without many good role models. But I'm proud of him, because he beat the odds. He found some positive examples along the way. He studied and achieved. Today he's contributing to our society in meaningful ways.

Not long ago, Shunton took my son Chance and me to a basketball game at the high school. As principal, he was a big shot. Everyone knew him and came up to talk to him. It was a pleasure to watch him relate well to the kids and parents who obviously appreciated him.

It was great to hang out with "the man" on campus. But something else made that night even more special.

It started in the parking lot, when some of his former students pulled up and got out of their car. They greeted him, and vice versa. Then Shunton nodded at me and said, "I want y'all to meet my dad."

He didn't say "father-in-law," but "dad." It rolled off his tongue like the most natural thing.

They said, "Wow, that's your dad?"

He said, "Yeah, and this here's my little brother, Chance."

You should have seen Chance beam! And there was a pretty good glow coming from yours truly, too!

I guess that's something I started years ago, when Shunton became close to my daughter. I started calling him "Son"—as in, "How's it goin', Son?" I knew he needed a father figure, and it just sort of happened that way.

Still, that night it was gratifying to hear him introduce me as his "dad." I really do think of him as my son.

It's an honor to be called a father. It's a title and a role to value, and to handle with care. I hope you find it more enjoyable and fulfilling than ever as you strive to be a Championship Father.

What Now?

It's a warm, sunny summer day in your neighborhood. The grass at the playground hasn't been mowed for a few weeks. The blades are long enough and thick enough to cushion the falls a little but short enough to let us run like the wind. (You do remember what it was like to run like the wind, right?)

That green field is a magnet for kids. The temperature is perfect for playing outside. You and I show up with lots of other guys for a game of—well, let's call it Championship Fathering.

It's time to choose up sides. I want to be on your team.

When it comes to your kids, you are the man! You make decisions every day that will result in their feeling deeply loved or not. You make coaching choices that will affect them now and forever. You model all kinds of values constantly for your children.

I know it can feel like too much—but you can do it. There's help available. That's one reason I'd like to be on your team. The National Center for Fathering stands ready to assist, and you can learn more about it on page 172.

In the meantime, I have a suggestion. It's a way you can start your quest for Championship Fathering. It's an exercise that especially fits Father's Day, making it a turnover day, ending one season and beginning another. But you can do it any day, even now.

We call it a Father's Day Review. It's a list of questions to ask yourself—and act on.

Part I: Evaluation of This Year

- What have I learned and practiced about loving my children and their mother this year?
- What have I learned and practiced about coaching my children this year?
- What have I learned and practiced about modeling for my children this year?
- What other children have I encouraged this year?
- What other dads have I asked to join me on the Championship Fathering team?

Part II: Planning for Next Year

- In what specific ways will I pursue improvement in loving my children and their mother next year?
- In what specific ways will I pursue improvement in coaching my children next year?
- In what specific ways will I pursue improvement in modeling for my children next year?
- What other children will I encourage in the coming year?
- What other dads will I ask to join me on the Championship Fathering team?

We're definitely looking at a deficit as we enter the next quarter of the game. But we can come back. We have to.

Keep practicing the fundamentals of Championship Fathering. That's the key to enjoying the privileges and responsibilities of being called "Dad."

Notes

Chapter 9

1. Albert Haynesworth press conference transcript, November 14, 2006, found at www.titansonline.com/news/newsmain_detail.php?PR Key=4349.
2. Samuel DeWitt Proctor, *The Substance of Things Hoped For: A Memoir of African-American Faith* (New York: G.P. Putnam's Sons, 1995), pp. 151-152.

Chapter 10

1. Werner Haug, et al, editors, "The Demographic Characteristics of Linguistic and Religious Groups in Switzerland," *The Demographic Characteristics of National Minorities in Certain European States, Population Studies*, vol. 2, no. 31 (Strasbourg: Council of Europe Directorate General III, Social Cohesion, January 2000). As quoted by Robbie Low, "The Truth about Men and the Church," at http://www.touchstone mag.com/archives/article.php?id=16-05-024-v.

Championship Fathering
A Call to Action

You've read about the crisis of fatherlessness and the negative consequences for children and for our society. Even if you're an involved dad, your children and grandchildren will grow up in a culture full of unfathered kids, and *will* be affected!

Dads are a critical part of the solution, but we have to get involved. For the sake of our children and grandchildren and millions of other kids, we need to stand up and be counted.

The National Center for Fathering is calling every dad to make a commitment to practice the five elements of *Championship Fathering*: loving his children, coaching his children, modeling for his children, encouraging other children, and enlisting other men to join the *Championship Fathering* team.

Our goal is to recruit 6.5 million fathers—equal to 10 percent of the fathers in America. That's enough dads standing shoulder-to-shoulder to stretch from Boston to San Diego. We believe it's enough to create a culture of Championship Fathering and positively influence our children's future. We hope this vision challenges and inspires you.

Make a difference! Get in the game! Decide today to live the principles of *Championship Fathering*. To make your commitment, please visit fathers.com/cf.

About the National Center for Fathering

We believe every child needs a dad he or she can count on. The research is clear: children thrive when they have an involved father—someone who loves them, knows them, guides them, and helps them achieve their destiny. At the National Center for Fathering, we inspire and equip men to be the involved fathers, grandfathers, and father figures their children need.

In response to the dramatic trend toward fatherlessness in America, Dr. Ken Canfield founded the National Center as a nonprofit, scientific, educational organization. Today the Center provides practical, research-based training and resources that equip men in virtually every fathering situation to be the involved fathers their children need.

The Center reaches more than one million dads annually through seminars, small-group training, the WATCH D.O.G.S. (Dads Of Great Students) program, our daily radio broadcast, and award-winning Web site and weekly e-mail. Our long-term goal is to create a culture of Championship Fathering by encouraging 10 percent of dads to commit themselves to fulfilling the tenets of Championship Fathering.

We focus our work in these four areas:

Research

At the core of all the National Center's work is the Personal Fathering Profile, a proprietary assessment tool that helps men understand their strengths and opportunities as fathers. Developed by a team of researchers led by the Center's founder, Ken R. Canfield, Ph.D., the Profile provides insights for fathers and serves as the benchmark for evaluating the effectiveness of our father-training programs. The Center continues to partner with researchers and practitioners interested in expanding the knowledge base of the fathering field. Contact dads@fathers.com.

Training

The National Center for Fathering offers training through seminars, small groups, and train-the-trainer programs. We have reached over 80,000 fathers through our seminars and equipped more than 1,000 trainers to provide our research-based father training in their local communities. Men interested in joining the Center's team of trainers and father coaches should visit www.fathers.com/training.

Programs

The Center provides leading-edge, turnkey fathering programs that others can easily implement. At this writing more than 1,000 schools in 32 states have WATCH D.O.G.S. programs. Visit www.fathers.com/watchdogs to learn about starting a program in your local school. The Center also offers a Championship Fathering small-group study as a companion to this book.

Resources

Our Web site at fathers.com provides a wealth of free resources for men in nearly every fathering situation—including new dads, granddads, divorced dads, stepfathers, adoptive dads, and father figures. Dads who make a commitment to Championship Fathering receive a weekly e-mail full of timely and practical tips on fathering. We also have a daily radio program that airs on more than 600 stations; selected programs can be downloaded from the Web site as podcasts.

The National Center for Fathering operates with support from individuals, foundation and corporate grants, and earned income from contracts and resource sales. For more information about the National Center, visit www.fathers.com/aboutus.

FOCUS ON THE FAMILY®

Welcome to the Family

Whether you purchased this book, borrowed it, or received it as a gift, we're glad you're reading it. It's just one of the many helpful, encouraging, and biblically based resources produced by Focus on the Family® for people in all stages of life.

Focus began in 1977 with the vision of one man, Dr. James Dobson, a licensed psychologist and author of numerous best-selling books on marriage, parenting, and family. Alarmed by the societal, political, and economic pressures that were threatening the existence of the American family, Dr. Dobson founded Focus on the Family with one employee and a once-a-week radio broadcast aired on 36 stations.

Now an international organization reaching millions of people daily, Focus on the Family is dedicated to preserving values and strengthening and encouraging families through the life-changing message of Jesus Christ.

Focus on the Family MAGAZINES

These faith-building, character-developing publications address the interests, issues, concerns, and challenges faced by every member of your family from preschool through the senior years.

| FOCUS ON THE FAMILY MAGAZINE | FOCUS ON THE FAMILY CLUBHOUSE JR.™ Ages 4 to 8 | FOCUS ON THE FAMILY CLUBHOUSE® Ages 8 to 12 | FOCUS ON THE FAMILY CITIZEN® U.S. news issues |

For More INFORMATION

 ONLINE:
Log on to
FocusOnTheFamily.com
In Canada, log on to
FocusOnTheFamily.ca

 PHONE:
Call toll-free:
800-A-FAMILY
(232-6459)
In Canada, call toll-free:
800-661-9800

Rev. 12/08